Deaf in DC

DEAF IN DC

A Memoir

MADAN VASISHTA

GALLAUDET UNIVERSITY PRESS
Washington, DC

Gallaudet University Press
Washington, DC 20002
http://gupress.gallaudet.edu

Library of Congress Cataloging-in-Publication Data

Vasishta, Madan, 1941–
  Deaf in DC : a memoir / Madan Vasishta.
      p. cm.
  ISBN-13: 978-1-56368-481-4 (pbk. : alk. paper)
  ISBN-10: 1-56368-481-0 (pbk. : alk. paper)
  1. Vasishta, Madan, 1941– 2. Deaf—Washington (D.C.)—Biography.
I. Title.
  HV2561.W17V38 2010
  362.4'2092—dc22
  [B]   2010045526

♾ The paper used in this publication meets the minimum requirements of
American National Standard for Information Sciences—Permanence of Paper
for Printed Library Materials, ANSI Z39.48–1984.

CONTENTS

Deaf in DC

1

The Story So Far . . .

AT THE AGE OF ELEVEN WHEN I WAS ATTENDING SIXTH grade and living in Gagret, a small village in northern India, I was stricken with mumps and typhoid and became deaf overnight. I thought I had died and gone to hell. I had never met a deaf person in my short life and not being able to hear made me feel less than human. The school I was attending seemed to agree with me on this demotion and discharged me. The idea of a deaf person attending school just did not enter in anyone's mind. That included me. Fortunately or unfortunately, no one in my family and circle of acquaintances knew about schools for the deaf. So there I was—a young deaf boy with no future and less hope.

That was in 1952. The idea of spending the whole life as a *behra* (Urdu equivalent of "dummy") for the rest of life didn't seem very palatable. My father, whom we all called Babuji, listened to all kind of "expert" advice and decided that deafness was a sickness since it was tied to typhoid and mumps. Like other sicknesses, it should be able to be cured. He tried all kind of remedies—regular Western doctors, ayurvedic (traditional Indian) medicine, *hakeems* practicing Greek medicine and, most of all, faith healers of all varieties. All of them gave me drugs in various shapes, sizes, and colors as well as cure-all ashes blessed by "holy men" that are found in every village. Needless to say, none of these worked, and, as I write this book about sixty years later, I am still deaf.

Seeing that no cures were working and I couldn't go to school, Babuji suggested that I should start working on our farm along with the servants. No one in our family had ever worked on the farm. We were landlords. My deafness had helped me win this "privilege." I started out as a cattle herder that required me to drive cattle a few miles away to one or the other pastures and watch over them all day long. I also had to cut grass, milk water buffaloes, and cows; collect and carry cow dung; and

I

carry water from the well for the family. Later, I was promoted to plowing the fields behind a pair of oxen and weeding and reaping wheat, corn, rice, and sugarcane.

My nine years working on the farm were pure hell. I hated every minute of it but managed to survive by my being a hopeless and unashamed optimist. I kept hoping that I would start my journey to become a successful person. What "success" entailed was never clear to me.

However, none of this stopped my education. My parents encouraged me to study on my own. Each year, as my elder brother Sham, who was a year ahead of me in school, moved on to the next class, I inherited his used textbooks. I spent every free minute with these textbooks. Reading came naturally to me and my problem was being unable to stop reading. I would finish the textbooks assigned for the whole year in a week. History and other subjects that depended on reading were also a cinch. For mathematics, I had to depend on sporadic tutoring by my brothers Sham and Narain. The big problem was learning English. In India at that time, instruction in English began during the fifth grade. I had the fortune of learning the alphabet and some basic English sentences such as "Mohan puts on a shirt." However, I wanted to learn English and learn it well as it was the ticket to big things.

I wrote down each grammatical construction that I could think of in Hindi and had Narain, my eldest brother, write down English equivalents. These were simple sentences like "I go," "I am going," "I have been going," and so forth. I started to make English sentences using Hindi language as a base. I would look at whatever I saw and try to describe it in English in my head. "That ox blue is" and correct it to "that ox is blue" after consulting my chart. This helped me get a good grasp of English grammar. Reading English books (mostly cowboy novels) using a dog-eared dictionary helped me build vocabulary. I read Jane Austen's *Pride and Prejudice* in several months. All of these haphazard approaches to education helped me improve my English and learn Sanskrit, mathematics, and other subjects. Seeing my progress, Babuji suggested I should take the high school examination. In 1957 I was a high school graduate, still herding cattle and plowing fields. My real education was mostly from reading all kind of books, any books that I could find. Since there was no library around, I had to walk as far as thirty miles to buy books from a junk shop.

I hoped that my education would be my ticket out of Gagret. However,

I also did think about becoming a *sadhu* (holy man), a cleaner, or an assistant to some truck driver, as farming was not exactly my cup of tea.

· The "ship" showed up in 1961 when Narain, my elder brother who lived in Delhi, learned about a photography school for the deaf being opened there. I jumped at the chance, and I packed a small bag and rode the train to Delhi the same day. After a stint working in a printing press, I joined the Photography Institute for the Deaf. This is where I met other deaf people for the first time and saw them using signs. I could not believe two people could communicate by moving their hands around. The two deaf guys refused to teach me signs as if it was a national secret. After some initial frustrations, I was able to make friends with my classmates. Within a week, I was signing fairly well. A whole new world opened for me.

During the next two years, I learned photography and sign language and also learned about deaf people, though not necessarily in that order. I got immersed within the Deaf community slowly as I became a fluent signer. After I earned my diploma in photography in two years, I started to teach in the same school. At the same time, I became a leader both in the Deaf and Dumb Association of Delhi and the All India Federation of the Deaf. More than that, I learned there was life after deafness and it was a good one.

Then another opportunity knocked. On encouragement from Narain, I applied for a government job as a technical photographer. This was a long shot and I was hesitant. However, I managed to pass the technical part of the examination with high marks, got the interview, and got the job. Getting a job in a stiff competition with about seventy hearing people helped me become a "successful" deaf person in the Delhi area. I had it made, so I thought. The next three years were great as I worked in a nice job, had a huge network of friends—both deaf and hearing—and rose as a leader among deaf people in Delhi and India.

The next logical step, of course, was getting married. Following the Indian tradition, I was betrothed by an arrangement made by relatives. It was decided that I would get married in a couple of years and then settle down in Delhi. However, something else was in store for me.

A deaf American lady, Hester Bennet, wrote to the office of the All India Federation of the Deaf asking for help in visiting Delhi in 1966. Since I was one of the few people fluent in English, Mr. B. G. Nigam, the general secretary, asked me to show the deaf lady around. For two days, very proudly, I took her around Delhi showing her the historical sites.

She did not know Indian signs and I did not know any American. So we communicated using pen and paper and some gestures for two days. On the second day, she asked me why I did not attend Gallaudet College. I could not believe there was a college for the deaf. The very next day, I went ahead and applied for admission.

In 1967, two important things happened in my life. I got married and moved to the United States to attend college.

My marriage to Nirmala (Nikki) was arranged by my aunt, Babuji's younger sister. Arranged marriage was the norm in India at that time. Unlike American couples, we had not fallen in love. We had not even dated. Actually, we had not even met each other. We both married strangers in February 1967 following the traditional Hindu ceremony, which lasted three days.

The saga of my coming to the United States after my admission to Gallaudet College is long and arduous. I was accepted and granted a full scholarship that covered tuition and room and board. However, I had to pay for books and unit fees, which amounted to $250. Due to stringent foreign exchange rules at that time, I had to have this amount in dollars and not in rupees. I wrote to Hester Bennet and she contacted Byron B. Burnes, then president of the National Association of the Deaf. Mr. Burnes wrote me a letter offering that amount and explained that he had deposited a check for $250 with Mr. Philips, the dean of students at Gallaudet. I thought the problem was resolved. However, this did not satisfy the Indian foreign ministry bureaucrats. This was a personal letter and they wanted an official letter from Gallaudet College. A letter from India to the United States took two weeks to arrive and sometimes more. Each exchange of letter between me and Mr. Burnes or Mr. Philips took almost a month. However, it was much faster compared to the Indian bureaucracy. It took my brother Narain and me a whole month of pounding doors outside various offices to finally get the needed documents that would allow me to apply to the U.S. embassy for a student visa.

The story here begins with my arrival in Washington, DC, on September 14, 1967.

2

Arrival in America

AIRPLANES, TO ME WHILE HERDING CATTLE IN GAGRET, looked like birds, a bit larger than a crow and the same size as a vulture. Later, when living in Delhi, I had the opportunity to see some of them at the airport. They were larger, much larger. I saw scores of people disappear into the belly of the "bird." However, the closest I had gotten to an airplane was the visitor's gallery at the airport. I longed for the moment when I would also ride an airplane. Now, I was actually flying in a plane. I hoped the plane would fly over Gagret so that I could look down to see how small the cows looked.

Sitting on the airplane felt funny. There was no sign of the heat or humidity that was suffocating the airport outside. The faint aroma of hot cooked food wafting from the galley reminded me that I was hungry. The combination of many emotions—excitement, worry, sadness, fear—had pushed the basic human need, hunger, to the background. I wished the plane would fly and those pretty air hostesses dressed in colorful silk saris would serve food.

No one had bothered to tell me if the plane was going directly to London or would stop on its way. I had not asked, either. I sat in the cramped seat next to a young lady who tried to talk to me and, on finding I was deaf, wrote, "Do you know if we are flying over Amritsar now?" She must have been from Amritsar. I looked outside the window. All I could see was white clouds. But in order to look knowledgeable, I said, yes, we were flying over Amritsar. I didn't feel guilty for lying. I had made someone happy.

The plane stopped in Tehran, Rome, and Frankfurt before arriving in London. A cab whisked me away to a small hotel, courtesy of Air India, in the city. The hotel room was the cleanest I had ever stayed in and the bed was the most comfortable I had slept in. However, sleep I could not.

I tossed and turned all night thinking about Gallaudet College and wondering how things would be there. How would they treat me? What was I going to do when my $50 ran out? That was more than my salary for a month as a photographer in India, but it would not go far in the United States. This was the amount allowed in foreign exchange and that I had received using money from my savings and an uncle's gift. Would I be able to keep up with other students? These thoughts scared sleep away. I was also thinking about Big Ben, the London Bridge, Piccadilly Circus, Hyde Park, and all of those places I had read about and seen in photographs. I wanted to see them all. However, I had only a few hours the next morning. At about five in the morning, I got tired of trying to sleep and got up; showered; dressed in the same suit, shirt, and tie I had worn during the flight; and found my way to the dining room. There was no one there except a waiter. He asked me how I liked my eggs. That was a strange question. Eggs to me were eggs. The only words related to eggs I knew were "boiled" and "omelet." So I asked for an omelet and he asked what kind. I didn't know the types of omelets but also didn't want to show my ignorance, so told him with the air of someone who specialized in omelets, I want an egg omelet. Later, I learned he had given me scrambled eggs.

After a hearty breakfast, I approached the concierge and asked him how to get to Piccadilly Circus. He wrote down directions for getting to the tube station and which station to go to from there and what to do after I got out. He was thorough. Armed with his instructions, I visited several sites in London without getting lost.

It was a surreal experience thinking I was one of those people who had seen all of those famous landmarks. When I worked in the Goyle Photography Studio, I had developed photographs showing people standing in front of various London landmarks. I was jealous of them. Now, I was there! I walked with a swagger. I wished I could get myself photographed in front of one of the monuments to send home. I didn't have a camera and I didn't know anyone with a camera within a five thousand miles radius. At that thought I smiled: my world was broadening.

But those landmarks were not what I had expected. Trafalgar Square was full of statues and, surprise, pigeons. There was nothing about Lord Nelson and his glorious naval victory. Hyde Park was just a park and Piccadilly Circus was a busy marketplace not much different than Connaught Place in New Delhi. I didn't let myself admit that these places had a halo effect because of what I had read about them.

The concierge had told me to be back before 1:00 p.m. for a ride to the airport. I made it fifteen minutes before that. I was hungry and asked for lunch. No, he said, the airline had paid for my breakfast only. I had to wait and eat in the plane or buy my own food. Having already read the menu in the morning, I decided to skip the lunch. I already had spent more than $4 in tube and admissions. My funds were dwindling fast. It was time to tighten the belt, literally.

It was a crisp fall day when the TWA plane I had boarded in London landed at Dulles Airport in Virginia. I had a splitting headache and the bright fall sun made my eyes water. I lined up behind other passengers for customs and immigration checks. I was not sure what lay ahead, and in order to avoid making any mistake, I looked around for any instructions on how to go through immigration. There were none. A lady with a clipboard caught my attention. She would look at her clipboard and shout something as she scanned the passengers in the line. I decided to go read for myself what she was telling us. After gesturing to the passenger behind me to watch my attaché case and bag, I walked to where the lady stood. I maneuvered behind her and looked at her clipboard. It was a list of passengers, and I saw my name encircled in red ink with the word "DEAF" written next to it. I tapped the woman and pointed at my name. She looked relieved. Apparently she was yelling my name in the hope that the deaf guy would hear her.

She was of great help. After learning that I could not lipread, she used a pencil and paper to tell me that she was going to help me go through immigration and customs. I didn't have to stand in the line. Deafness has its advantage. She took me to a closed counter and talked to the supervisor, who looked through my passport and stamped it with a smile. I thought about the rude, slow, and unfriendly immigration personnel I had dealt with in New Delhi compared to their U.S. counterparts. The efficiency, friendliness, and the "may I help you?" attitude were simply overwhelming.

Then she took me to the baggage claim area. The luggage carousel fascinated me. Bags of all shapes and sizes were going around and around and people were picking up their bags. There were no coolies—the ever present laborers who carried bags in India, Americans seem to do all their work themselves. We waited for my little bag to make its appearance. Finally the carousel stopped, and I learned that my bag was still somewhere between India and the United States. With the clipboard lady's help, I filled out the forms they gave us, picked up my tote bag and small attaché case, and walked outside. I paid $2.50 to the driver of the airport bus that was to take me to Washington, DC.

Up until then, my vision of America consisted of cowboys trotting on their sorrels and pintos through the purple sage and mesquite. I also had seen some movies starring Gary Cooper, John Wayne, and others riding fast horses, shooting guns, cleaning up towns of black-hatted bad guys, and riding into the sunset for yet another adventure. The lush Virginia countryside along the Dulles access road was very different than the America I had envisioned. Imagine my disappointment at not seeing any cowboys or horses. There were, however, more important things to worry about, and I decided to forget the missing cowboys and horses for now.

I had about $43 in my pocket, two pairs of clothes, a pair of shoes, and the clothes on my back. I didn't know anyone in the whole country and didn't even have a letter of introduction. There was little or no hope in my mind of getting the bag containing all my worldly possessions— two suits, four shirts and four pairs of pants, underwear, and socks. A few gifts for people who might help me completed the contents of my small bag. It was all gone.

The bus dropped me at 12th Street, NW. And now I faced the problem of getting to Gallaudet. I tried to talk to people like I always did in India but found no one understood me. A huge black porter was helpful. He asked me to write. In the past, hearing people had always written to me and I always responded with my voice because I was understood. I never had to write to express myself. This was a new experience. My speech was not good in America! I had never heard English spoken, especially by an American; therefore I had no idea, and still do not, how Americans speak. My heavy Gagret accent had made my speech unintelligible in America.

The cab driver and the porter didn't know where Gallaudet College was. I gave them the address and the cab driver shook his head and drove away after taking a look at it. Apparently, Gallaudet College was not situated in an area that cab drivers liked to go. The helpful porter made getting the cab for me his personal mission. He waved for another and talked to the cab driver who opened the back door for me. As the cab drove, I noticed the difference between Indian and American cabs and drivers. The driver sat relaxed and used the index finger of his right hand to steer. I didn't know about power steering, so I wondered how strong his index finger was. As he stopped at a light and then started again, I was puzzled, as he never shifted gears. I craned my head and noticed there was no clutch, either. American cars and drivers were funny, I thought.

I had practiced the American Manual Alphabet on the airplane and felt very comfortable with the speed I could spell. I was confident that I would be able to communicate with American deaf people easily and flexed my fingers.

The cab entered Gallaudet campus and the cab driver stopped in front of a huge building, which I later learned was College Hall. I saw about thirty students milling around, signing to each other with the speed of lightning. The cabdriver asked me where I wanted to get off. I told him this place would be fine and got out. I stood there with the Air India handbag at my feet and gaped at the students walking and running around signing so animatedly. I could not understand even one word. I decided to keep my knowledge of the American Manual Alphabet a secret.

The students ignored me totally, and I wondered if I was invisible. In India, the arrival of a stranger is a big event. A student from another country would have been surrounded by and questioned about where he was from and what he was doing there. I looked at myself to make sure I was there and knew that I had to do something to get help or I would have to stand there with the Air India handbag and the attaché case at my feet for the rest of my life.

My first two attempts to get someone's attention were a total failure. I waved my hand to a tall, thin guy who looked at me for a second. He walked toward me and I began to spell, "W-H-E-R-E." By the time I was spelling "R" he was gone back to his friends. My effort to get the attention of another guy met with the same fate. The first thing I learned about Gallaudet students was that they have little or no patience with someone who does not sign. I thought this was rude, but then I remembered the kind of treatment deaf people without the ability to speak clearly get when they are trying to get attention of a hearing person. "Well," I told myself, "the tables are turned here." However, the irony was I was also deaf. But I was a deaf person who didn't know American signs.

Finally, I did succeed in getting the attention of two pretty girls. They both had short hair, wore tee shirts and shorts, and seemed like they were just going for a walk. I waved timidly and was surprised to see them both stop in their tracks and look at me with interest. One of them looked at the Air India bag on the ground and pointed at it and then at me. I nodded my head vigorously. We were communicating!

My "w-h-e-r-e" was interrupted again, however. One of the girls grabbed my hand and turned it around to face her. I was first puzzled, but then the light dawned upon me. I was spelling the letters to myself. It was like someone showing a photograph to another person but keeping it facing himself! Boy, did I feel dumb. Spelling in this new orientation of the hand was a bit difficult at first but became easier in a few minutes.

Then the second girl spread the five fingers of her left hand and touched her pinky and ring finger with the index finger of her right hand alternately and pointed at me with a questioning look in her eyes. She wanted to know if I was a pinky or a ring finger person. I shrugged my shoulders like I had seen Americans shrug in the movies. My shrug must have been pretty awkward—it was my first shrug.

One of them wrote on her notebook, "Are you a freshman or prep?" I didn't know which one I was. Worse still, I didn't know what a prep or freshman was. Our talk, or rather the effort to talk, got the attention of a male student with thick glasses hanging from the very tip of his nose. The three consulted with each other and then the male student motioned me to follow him. I waved to the two girls and followed my benefactor.

He wrote on paper that his name was Godsey and he was from Florida. "Where are you from?" He wrote. I pointed at the Air India bag. He nodded his head in understanding.

We passed the College Hall and walked to another building. He wrote, "This is Fowler Hall." I wondered why he called the buildings halls. A hall in British English is a large room and a building is a building. But I had more important things to worry about than the nomenclature so I remained quiet. Fowler Hall, it turned out, was a dormitory for preparatory boys. Godsey, my guide, knocked on a door and a muscular man opened it. They both exchanged conversation with fingers and hands flying to and fro. I looked from one to other and began to talk to the new person, who looked back at me as if I was speaking Greek. Apparently, he didn't understand one word I was saying. Their exchange in signs was also Greek to me; I could not understand even one word. Their conversation resulted in the other man's handing me a key along with a pillowcase and two bed sheets. Godsey and I climbed four floors and then he led me to a room—his own—and helped me make one of the beds. I learned later that he had offered to be my roommate until the mystery of my being a pinky or a ring finger was resolved. The bed-making process was new for me. I had never made a bed and was glad for his help. In India, one spread a *duree*—a thin mat—and a bed sheet over the cot. There was no tucking needed as there was no mattress to tuck the sheets under. This tucking the sheet, I thought, was a bit too much. I would rather let the sheets hang out.

Hunger was gnawing at my arteries. I made the universal sign for eating. He shook his head. The cafeteria was already closed. We walked to yet another building. It was the Students Union Building (SUB), he told me. My brother Narain was very active in the student union in his college and later in the railway employees union. I thought about joining the students union later when I was settled.

In the student union building, I saw my first vending machine. Godsey helped me insert a dollar in the change machine and then helped me find a dime and a nickel. I inserted the two coins in the Coke machine and pressed a button. I got a can of Coke and was pleasantly surprised to find the can very cold. The vending machine had a refrigerator built into it. I was amazed. I also got a package of biscuits, which Godsey called cookies. While munching cookies and sipping the Coke, I looked around. Godsey pointed to a machine in the corner. I walked to it with coins in my hand, as I was still hungry. There didn't seem to be any food in that machine and I looked helplessly at Godsey. He wrote, "This is a pinball machine. Later you can play on it." The steel balls in that machine didn't look very edible, anyway.

The Coke and the biscuits, I mean cookies, gave me some energy and we walked back to Fowler Hall. Godsey showed me the bathroom where I changed into my sleeping suit, shook hands with Godsey, who looked puzzled, slowly got into the bed, and passed out.

3

The Cafeteria

THE NEXT MORNING, I WOKE UP AFTER TWELVE HOURS OF dreamless sleep. I felt much better and was ready to face my life in the new country. I saw Godsey sitting in a chair. He smiled when he saw me awake and signed, "EAT." I was indeed hungry and it was nice of him to remember I had gone to bed hungry the night before. I got up and walked to him and shook his hands and went to take a hurried shower and dressed in my suit and the tie to go eat breakfast. Godsey, who was dressed in a t-shirt and shorts, didn't say anything. He was a very understanding guy.

My visit to the Gallaudet cafeteria was an American experience. The stainless steel equipment and floors, that were so clean that you could eat sitting on it, amazed me. However, the thing that really got my attention was the number of machines that dispensed various sodas, three kinds of fruits juices, and milk. One could fill his glass with all the milk or other drink that one wanted. In India, you were given measured amounts of everything. If you wanted more, it was a flat no. I had read in history books how rivers of milk used to flow in ancient India. However, I had not read that there were countries where these rivers were still flowing and there were several other rivers in addition to the river of milk. There were rivers of Coke and orange juice. I knew the United States was rich, but reading about prosperity is one thing and to experience it is something else. It is just like you have to experience poverty to get the real feeling about being poor.

The buffet wafted an aroma of cooked eggs and some new things. I copied Godsey and took a tray and added two glasses and silverware to it and followed him in the serving line. I got an omelet, which I learned later was scrambled eggs. I said no to bacon and sausage and accepted a couple of slices of toasted bread. Godsey opted for some round brown chapatis and poured thick syrup on them. I was not brave enough to try them. Then, I learned how to ply the milk machine. The milk was ice cold. I wondered if I could get it boiled. Since there was no stove around and everyone appeared to drink the milk cold, I decided to follow suit.

While eating my first American breakfast, I looked at other students trying to understand what they were signing and understood nothing. Godsey introduced me to the two students sitting at the table. They signed something and the only sign I understood was whether I was a freshman or prep. I shook my head and shrugged my shoulders to indicate the limbo status I was in. They went back to talking to each other. I got the feeling that this class status was very important. The "first-year student" that is used in India and other countries to denote a class placement was not going to work here.

Godsey patiently spelling each word slowly told me that after the breakfast we would go to see the dean of students. I hoped a visit to the dean would help clarify where I stood. Since conversation was cumbersome with me, Godsey began to talk to other students at the table, and I began to survey the dining hall. I wondered which one of these students would become my best friend and which one would hate my guts. I tried to guess, but it was hard.

A student caught my attention as he poured himself four glasses of milk and one of orange juice. His tray also held a stack of those brown chapatis, which I later learned were pancakes, bacon, and a heap of hash brown potatoes. I was hungry, but I was sure that I could not eat half of what he had and then drink four glasses of milk. The guy was big and I was curious to see how he was going to finish his enormous breakfast. The real shocker came when I saw him eat half his breakfast and drink one glass of milk. The remaining food and the three glasses of cold milk went down the drain in the dishwashing area! I thought of all the little kids clamoring for milk back home in India and other countries and felt guilty as I looked at my breakfast tray. I was already full, but I forced myself to finish everything.

4

Prep or Freshman?

SINCE IT WAS EARLY AND THE DEAN'S OFFICE WAS NOT open, Godsey took me around the SUB. He introduced me to the students he knew. I had met many Americans in India—they were all "Americans." Here, however, they were not from America; they were from Florida, California, New York, and other states! Of course, I was from India; nobody asked about Himachal Pradesh or Punjab.

Godsey walked me to what he called the Hall Memorial Building. I wondered if the right name was Memorial Building Hall but didn't ask. Dean Phillips's office was the first room as we entered the building. Godsey talked to the secretary who took me into the dean's office as Godsey waved a farewell to me. Dean Phillips was tall and gaunt and peered at me from behind his glasses. I clasped my hands to say "namaste," the traditional Indian greeting, but saw Dean Phillips's quizzical look and moved my hands quickly to my sides. After trying to sign something, he gave up and wrote on a piece of paper, "You are two weeks late." As if I didn't know that. If only he knew how I had to spend more than two weeks wandering around the corridors of Indian bureaucracy with my elder brother Narain! I started to explain the reason, spelling slowly, but he waved both his hands in front of him to make me stop. Then I asked him the most important question by touching the pinky and ring finger with my right index finger. He looked at my file and touched his ring finger. Now I knew I was a freshman and felt relieved like a person who has finally learned about his identity. He then wrote on the paper that I must go get my physical and register today in another room in the same building and also to get my ID card.

Following Dean Phillips's instructions, I walked across the campus back to Fowler Hall. There was a small hospital there, but they called it the infirmary. The "infirmary" was bustling with students who were anything but infirm. Presiding over the students was a tall, beautiful woman in a white nurse's uniform. This was Donna. She was not a nurse but, as I learned later, the receptionist there. She carried a clipboard and signed to each student making notes. I watched Donna as she worked. The most interesting thing about her was her smile. It never left her face. She smiled narrowly or very broadly, but she kept smiling. That made me think of a hospital, any hospital, in India. The receptionist, if there was one, gave you dirty looks and made you sit and wait. The nurses were rude and the doctors condescending. Donna was very different. It was a very novel American experience for me.

I had to show my sealed envelope with my chest X-rays and other medical information to ensure that my living in America would not endanger other people. The U.S. embassy had already checked that out, but for some reason, it had to be done again here. Donna took my envelope and seeing that I didn't understand signs, wrote that I should wait and all would be taken care of. I read her note and looked up at her and she gave me a 220-watt smile.

A student with some bandages on his face was the only person who looked infirm in the infirmary. He was signing very fast to some students. From some of the gestures he made, I understood he was explaining how he had gotten hurt. Since he used the gesture for driving a car, I assumed he had a car accident and thought of hundreds of Americans who died in car accidents.

After he had related the story a couple of times to different groups, the student noticed me. He began to spell using the British Manual Alphabet when he learned I didn't know American signs. He was Hartmut from Germany. His class ranking was index finger, so he has been here for two years. Slowly and painstakingly, he told me how his car had hit a side rail resulting in his face being banged on the steering wheel. I tried to tell him to be careful in the future. He shook his head. It was not his fault, he told me, and he berated the traffic and stupid drivers. I learned that day that all auto accidents are other people's fault even when one hits a stationary object.

After submitting the report from the infirmary to Dean Phillips's office I looked for Godsey to tell him about my ring finger status, but he had gone away. So I walked around the hallway looking for the room where I had to register. I had thought it would take me five minutes to sign my name in some "register" and be on my way. But there was a long line outside the room. First they had to check if I had paid my tuition and other dues, which was not hard. After learning my name, which I spelled slowly for them, the very efficient people worked fast, and I had a receipt saying I had paid for everything. I looked at the amount on the receipt showing what I had "paid" and soon figured out that it was more than my two years' salary at the National Physical Laboratory where I had worked until four days earlier. The fact that this money was paid from the grant-in-aid and scholarship money that was awarded to me didn't deter me from squaring my shoulders and puffing out my chest. I was in the big league!

The next step was picking the courses I was to take that semester. I had thought, like colleges in India, everything was decided for you. Here I could choose what I was going to study. That was hard for me to believe and harder still to decide what I was going to study. Seeing my dilemma, the registrar got a student assistant to help me. The student pointed at herself and spelled M-A-R-Y slowly and then touched her left index finger with her right index finger. Well, it was obvious she was neither a prep nor a freshman. I copied her index finger to index finger sign and looking at her with my eyebrows raised. She wrote, "I am a junior." I was not sure if junior was lower than prep or higher, but I decided not to show my ignorance.

Mary worked with me with great patience. She told me that I had to choose one science class, one history class, and so forth. I decided on chemistry because Ramesh, my cousin, had majored in chemistry and was teaching this subject in the Punjab University. It was a bit humiliating to think that Ramesh, who is six months younger than me, was teaching college while I was just starting college. I was back on earth and my shoulders and chest shrank back to its normal size.

With the help of Mary, I was able to fill out a schedule card. I selected football for PE and was excited about playing football. Wow, that would be fun. Little did I know what I was getting myself into.

After registration, which took more than two hours, I was directed to a building called the "old counseling center" to get an identification card. I wondered why it didn't have a "hall" before or at the end of its name. Perhaps, I thought, Old Counseling Center Hall was too long a name for such a small building.

I showed my receipt to a guy downstairs where they had set up a camera on a tripod and were taking photographs for the identification cards. I looked at everything they had and was impressed with the expensive 35-mm camera and the lights. I thought it would be fun to work here, but then I admonished myself that I was a student now and had finished my work as a photographer.

As I came up from the basement photo room, I ran into Godsey. He had been looking for me. His first question was about the two fingers. I touched my ring finger and he showed his joy by patting my back. I guessed a freshman was better than prep. He gestured to ask me if I wanted to look around the campus. I did and together we began to walk as he pointed toEly Hall, the library, Krug Hall, and Cogswell Hall. I noted that the library that was actually a huge hall was not called a hall.

Then he asked if I wanted to see American football. Of course I did and wondered what changes they had made to the game of football to call it "American football."

5

American "Football"

I LOVED PLAYING AND WATCHING FOOTBALL. IN GAGRET, I would walk as far as fifteen miles to go watch a football match. Here a football game was only a few steps away. It felt good to be living in a place where all the action was within walking distance. We arrived at the field and I looked at the twenty or more players dressed in uniforms and steel helmets. Americans always looked big to me, but dressed in the football gear, they looked huge. I made a mental note never to get any of them irritated at me so that I didn't have to deal physically with them. I wondered why they had all that gear and then saw the "football" was also of an odd shape. I sat with my new friend on the bleachers and waited for the action and excitement for which football is famous. I also wondered how they would be able to run with all that gladiator's gear.

There was something odd about this game. Half of the players would stand in a circle facing each other with their heads bowed and pray. The other players stood idly and looked bored. The group of players that had prayed in the circle then would line up facing the other players with one or both hands on their knees. Suddenly, everyone would be falling on each other or running in all directions except for where the football was. The football was thrown with a hand and no penalty was called. Then they would stop only to huddle and line up all over again. They continued doing that for a while and I got bored. I figured that they were trying to start the game but something was going wrong.

After waiting patiently for some action for about ten minutes, I asked Godsey, "When will they start to play?" As I mentioned before, he was a very understanding guy, however, my question must have pushed him to the brink. He shook his head and wrote, "They are playing." His face, however, clearly said, "Boy, are you dumb."

Then he stood up and gestured for me to follow him. As we walked, he slowly spelled and gestured to tell me that since I was a freshman, I had to move to another dormitory. We walked up the fourth floor to his room where I packed my bag and attaché case with my meager belongings and came down to return my key to the Fowler Hall supervisor, Mr. Martin. Ely Hall was only a hundred yards away and Godsey took me to the supervisor's office with glass walls on two sides. He explained my situation and the two guys who looked younger than me had a short discussion between them. They kept talking and looking at a register. Apparently, they had to decide which room to assign me. Finally, one of them gave me two bed sheets and a pillowcase and the other one handed me a key after I signed a receipt for it. One of them wrote "308" on a paper slip and pointed me toward the corridor. I shook hands with Godsey and took the staircase to the third floor. The door of 308 was locked, so I used my new key and slowly opened the door. A tall thin boy with pimples on his face and disheveled brown hair jumped from the bed. He had a book in his one hand and a smoking cigarette in the other. He looked at me for two seconds and at the attaché case and the bag, then threw the book on the bed and left without a word.

"He does not seem to be overly fond of me," I said to myself and stood there wondering what to do. Since one bed was bare, I threw the sheets on it, sat down and surveyed the room. It had bare floors and a large window with two panels on each side that were open. Two desks facing each other with chairs under them were next to the window. A dresser with a large mirror and two closets on both sides were built in. Two walls were bare except for a large poster of Clark Gable on one wall. He was standing leaning on a tree and smoking a cigarette. I saw something pasted on the cigarette in the poster and stood up for a closer examination. It was a small sticker with the message "The surgeon general has determined that cigarette smoking is hazardous for your health." "My new roommate, whoever and wherever he was, has a sense of humor," I thought.

I looked at Clark Gable, who was still smiling. Maybe he also thought that warning was funny. I was looking at the poster when the door opened and the young guy entered again. He came toward me with his hand extended and saying something. I shook his hand and told him I was deaf by putting my hand on my ears and shaking my head. He pointed his finger at me and gestured "SIGN." I shook my head again. He jabbed his lips with his index finger, "LIP READ?" That must have been exasperating for him. He looked around perhaps asking Clark Gable to help him and moved his index finger on his left palm in writing motion. I gave a vigorous yes. There was still something I knew. He found a pen on the dresser and wrote on a yellow pad, "My name is Dan and I am from Indiana." I took the pad and the pen from him and wrote, "My name is Madan and I am from India." We both examined our writing and both of us must have noticed "Dan" in "Madan" and "Indian" in "Indiana" as we both laughed at the same time and shook hands again.

With Dan in our dorm room.

6

First Day of Classes

NEXT MORNING, I GOT UP EARLY AND SAW THAT DAN WAS still asleep. I took a change of clothes, my bag of toiletries, and my small towel and went to the bathroom to get ready. There was no one in the bathroom, so I leisurely shaved and was ready to shower when I saw in the mirror two boys entering the bathroom and making it straight to the shower stall. I stopped shaving as both of them were stark naked. I couldn't see them in the mirror any more but could see the steam coming from the shower stall. I have never thought that two men could be naked in front of each other. In India, we used shorts or a small dhoti or loin cloth to cover ourselves when taking a bath in public.

My original plan was to use my shorts to bathe in and then dry them in my room. I decided to wait for the two guys to leave and took my time brushing my teeth. Momentarily, both guys came out drying themselves with their huge towels and signing to each other at the same time. I looked at my towel; it was less than half the size of theirs. I thought of hiding it, but they were not looking at my towel or me at all.

They produced their toilet kits, joined me on either side, and started to brush their teeth. All the time they kept their dialogue going, and, yes, they were still fully in the buff. Sandwiched between them, I was very uncomfortable and hurriedly washed my face, dried it and left the bathroom. The shower had to wait.

I dressed up in my suit and tie, used mustard oil in my hair and combed it so that each strand was in place. After checking my schedule, I picked up the books that were needed for the day and made my way to the cafeteria. There were a few students eating there and I wondered when they would get ready for the classes that were to begin in fifteen minutes. After eating my breakfast hurriedly, I walked to the Hall Memorial Building (HMB) to start my first day as a student. I was exhilarated. The last time

I had sat in an academic class was in December of 1951, almost sixteen years ago. I was a student again.

The main door of the HMB didn't yield to my pulls and pushes. I went around and tried the side door. Same result. It was 7:55 a.m., and I began to worry about being late for my class on the very first day. I looked around helplessly and saw a couple with arms around each other coming from the upper-class dormitories. They must have seen my efforts to open the door and came to me and began to sign, which I didn't understand. The male student saw the schedule card on top my books and took it. After glancing at the card for less than five seconds, he showed me my schedule. I had classes from Monday to Friday. He pointed to Saturday and looked at me. I understood. It was a Saturday and they didn't have classes on Saturdays here. I had read the schedule many times, but the idea that all Saturdays were holidays never came to my mind.

Dan was still asleep when I returned to our room. I put the books away and was glad that I had two full days with nothing to do. But the problem was I had nothing to do, either. There were no friends to hang out with and no money to go see a movie or places to visit. I decided to take a walk.

Dressed in my suit and tie and walking on Florida Avenue in Northeast Washington, DC, I must have looked odd. I was not sure where I was going, but I hoped to find a marketplace where I could look at stores and do some window-shopping just to pass the time. Since I had no map, I decided to stay on the same road. At each block, I read the names of the streets and tried to remember them in case I got lost.

An interesting thing I noticed was that as I moved from block to block, the streets didn't have names; instead, they had numbers. I passed 7th, 6th, and 5th Streets on Florida Avenue. In India, all streets have names and if you wanted to go to an address, you had to ask around. I thought that was real smart. All streets intersecting Florida Avenue had numbers and I could easily figure out how to get to someone living on Florida Avenue in house number 453. That should be between 4th and 5th Streets. That was a revelation. Why didn't we do that in India? The street names do not leave any clue where a place is.

The other thing I noticed was that cars that sped by me were only a few inches from the end of the sidewalk. There were no bicycles or motorcycles; everyone drove a car. I did see some pedestrians, but they were rare. After walking about a mile, I remembered the great American tradition of hitchhiking. That would be fun, I thought.

I raised my thumb the way I had seen people doing in the movies thinking that, just like in the movies, a car would stop and pick me up. The cars, however, continued to speed by me. I stopped at the next crossing and waited for the light to turn red. Perhaps drivers of stopped cars might be more willing to offer a ride. This didn't work, either. The drivers would steal glances at me and look away. After four or five tries, I gave up and started walking again. What one sees in movies does not happen in real life.

Seeing a bus, I decided to ride one back to Gallaudet, as I was tired. I asked two young guys about a bus that might be going to Gallaudet. They pointed to a bus and I got into it. This bus, however, took me to Silver Spring in Maryland. From there, I had to change two buses to return to where I had taken the original bus. After that, there were going to be no more buses for me, and I stopped at the police station, got directions, and walked all the way back to Gallaudet. It was an adventure I could have done without.

I didn't have a class that day, but I did learn a lot. Hitchhiking, unlike in the movies, was not easy. A city can be laid out as a grid and not grow by itself as maze of narrow allies. This learning pattern continued during the next six years as a student at Gallaudet: most of my learning happened outside of the classroom.

7

Teachers and Students

The self taught man seldom knows anything accurately, and he does not know a tenth as much as he could have known if he had worked under teachers, and besides, he brags, and is the means of fooling other thoughtless people into going and doing as he himself has done.

—Mark Twain in "Taming the Bicycle"

SINCE MY DEAFNESS AND THE RESULTING DISMISSAL FROM school when I was in the sixth grade, I have been teaching myself, except for the stint in the photography school for the deaf in Delhi. Thus, Gallaudet was the first school I attended after a hiatus of sixteen years. I was thrilled. I was going to sit in a classroom and have my own books and several teachers were going to teach me.

On Monday, I got up at four in the morning, collected my bathing stuff, and made it to the bathroom. I wanted to shower before the hordes of nude boys invaded my privacy. I showered, shaved, and went back to bed, where I thought about India, my wife, relatives, and friends and got misty-eyed.

Promptly at 7:00, I got ready to go to the dining room for breakfast. Dan was still asleep. I wondered if I should wake him up because he also had a class at 8:00, but I decided against it as he was sleeping very soundly. There were few people eating breakfast. Later, I learned that more than half of the students didn't eat breakfast and some just grabbed a cup coffee. I ate leisurely and observed students as they signed to each other. I caught one or two signs and understood nothing.

I do not remember my first two classes. We were there for less than fifteen minutes and were excused after the teachers handed out syllabi and answered questions. I do remember my third class—English 101—because it was smaller, about seven or eight of us in that class. The professor, Mr. Terrence O'Rourke, signed very expressively and the students appeared to be captivated with his lecture. They asked questions and there appeared to be a lively discussion of which I was not a part. All I could do was look from face to face and smile when they smiled and frown when they frowned. I wondered what we were talking about and what the homework would be. I wrote on my notebook "What is our homework?" to show to the professor at the end of the class.

When the class ended, three students moved to the professor quickly. I stood behind them so they could ask their questions. There were no questions, however. To my horror, the three students took packs of cigarettes out of their pockets and put cigarettes to their lips. I thought the professor was going to yell at them for this lack of respect. One didn't smoke in front of elders, especially teachers, in India. Instead of yelling, Mr. O'Rourke took out his lighter and lighted their cigarettes as well as his own. The four of them continued talking while blowing smoke at each other. I almost forgot to ask about my homework.

Mr. O'Rourke read my note and asked one of the students something and went back to talking with the other two. This student took my notebook and wrote under it about the chapter we were to read. He also pointed out the syllabus showing the schedule for reading and other assignments. I should have read the syllabus first, I thought.

There were a total of fifteen hours of classes a week plus five hours of sign language classes. That left a lot of time for me to read for pleasure. So I visited the library and picked out two books. In Delhi, the local libraries allowed their patrons to borrow only one book at a time. The American library there allowed two books, which was really nice. I hoped that the Edward Miner Gallaudet (EMG) Library would also allow me to borrow two books at one time. Not that it mattered as the library was only about fifty yards from Ely Hall. I had never lived so close to a library in my life and felt that flying all the way to another hemisphere for such a privilege was worth it.

While I was looking for my books, I saw a girl go to the checkout counter with an armload of books. She dropped the books unceremoniously on the counter and stood there chewing gum while the librarian stamped the cards. The girl picked up the whole load—ten or so books—and walked out. That was baffling, so I walked to the librarian and wrote on a paper, "How many books can I check out?"

The librarian looked puzzled. "As many as you want," she wrote in reply and smiled. The librarians in India didn't smile. They scowled and acted as if the books were their personal property and the clients were trying to steal them.

Oh boy! As many books you want. I decided to be conservative and took out four books. I spent fifteen hours a week in classes, a little more doing homework, and the rest being neglected by the one-thousand-plus student body of Gallaudet. And, of course, I read books.

The homework and assignments were fun and the only problem I had was the chemistry class. I didn't even have general science in India and had opted for Sanskrit instead of science as I had no access to a laboratory at home. I spent more time on chemistry homework than all the other classes combined. Still, I was having a hard time keeping up.

The other class I was having a problem with was PE class, even though it had no homework. The problem was the class itself. We were learning how to play a game called "touch football" or "flag football." Actually, I was the only one who needed to learn; all the other students knew how to play this game as much as I knew how to play football, I mean soccer.

The lecture on football rules by Mr. Reynolds, the PE instructor who looked like a movie star, was beyond me as Mr. Reynolds signed fast like everyone else at Gallaudet. I asked Tom, one of the guys Dan had introduced me to, about the rules. He shook his head and said, "You will learn when we play." That made sense. I learned soccer rules while playing it and thought that Mr. Reynolds was wasting our time teaching us rules of the game. All students were eager to run out and play.

Play we did. Rather, the whole class, except for me, did after the first lecture. The class would meet in the football field. Mr. Reynolds would appoint two captains, who would then select their teams. I was always selected as the last player, and the expression on the face of the unlucky captain who had to "select" me loudly said, "I wish you were somewhere else." I would walk to where the team was and hide behind other players, which was not hard as all of them were a head taller than me.

Playing defense was not hard. The captain would make me stand in line and strike a pose for me to copy. I understood from his gestures that I had to stop whoever tried to cross the line. I never succeeded in my effort, however. The nimble and fast guys, who were all seven or eight years younger than me, easily bypassed me.

Playing offense was another issue. The captain would give instructions to all players feverishly. Each player had a specific role. At the end, he would point at me and to "run." That is what I understood. However, I would mix up defense with offense easily. Trying to defend was when I should have run and caught the ball. I would end up running here and there without knowing what I was doing.

I could not throw the ball; it wobbled and fell a few feet from me. Nor could I catch one. If the ball came my way, I would close my eyes hoping it would go away only to have it hit me in the head or chest or even lower. I was embarrassed and signed "SORRY" to my teammates.

Despite my dismal performance, no one ever laughed at me. In India, if there was a player who was performing at my level, all other players would have rolled on the grass laughing and jeering at him. These American young guys, some still in their teens, never laughed at me. The only reaction from them was either to look away at my gaffes or to pat me on the back. I was very thankful to this great American trait of not laughing at the weak.

While the lack of respect for teachers bothered me, I was amazed at the respect that teachers showed the students. In India, a teacher is a dictator in the classroom. He demands total obedience and gets it even from the most rebellious student. At Gallaudet, I noticed that teachers treated students as equals. Students felt comfortable in questioning the teachers and even challenging them on issues being discussed.

If a student didn't do his homework, the teacher in India would chastise him in front of the whole class. He would be called "stupid," "careless," and other names. His parents would be called names as well for producing such an irresponsible child. A student could be asked to leave the class and go home and not to return until he brought the homework with him.

The self-confidence and comfort that the students felt at Gallaudet was reassuring and also catching. I was not scared of teachers like I would have been in India. At the same time, I was not brave or brash enough to ask the teacher to light my cigarette. However, I did appreciate this consideration and felt comfortable in talking to teachers after class for information about homework and questions I had.

8

Reading Palms

BEING IGNORED BY EVERYONE JUST BECAUSE I COULD NOT
sign American bothered me. I wished there were some students who were
patient enough to talk to me by signing slowly so that I could learn to
sign. I kept wondering how I could make people communicate with me. I
was used to being the center of attention in Delhi and this experience of
"being invisible" was humiliating and depressing. I thought Americans
were unfriendly and arrogant.

The sign language class I was taking met five times a week and I was,
indeed, learning signs. But I felt I needed practice to improve my signing
speed, especially reading them. I gathered that knowing signs was not
enough; being able to read them as fast as one signed was very important.

Reading in a new written language, one could read slowly and go
back and reread the sentence or the whole paragraph if one didn't understand it. One could use the dictionary for new words. The book one was
reading had patience.

The problem with sign language is that one cannot "reread" signs.
The signer might be willing to repeat a sign or two, but asking him or her
to keep repeating everything he or she signed does not work. There is the
basic difference between a book and a human. Humans move and they
do not belong to you.

I needed a way to get good signers to sit patiently with me. Unfortu-
nately, all the students who had patience with me were novices like Dan.
Practicing signs with Dan was not an option as he, like me, preferred the
Olympia typewriter or the yellow legal pad.

The idea for getting some people to help me practice signs came from
Dan for a different reason. One evening while we were discussing various
aspects of Indian "culture" ("Gunga Din" and Goddess Kali being Dan's

favorites), Dan suddenly asked if I could read palms. India is famous for palm reading. No? Yes, I did. I knew palm reading!

I had "learned" to read palms for the same reason—talking to people. I had read in an Indian annual almanac, not very different from the *Farmer's Almanac* in the United States, about reading palms. There was an illustration of a palm with all of those lines and what they supposedly stood for. I had checked my own palm using the guidelines given in the almanac. Since I was only about thirteen years old at that time and had the whole future ahead of me, I could not really tell if my future as indicated by the guidelines was correct or not. Everything was pretty vague except for the "life line." It started from the bottom of the pinkie finger and ended between the middle and the index finger—that is, if the owner of the hand was going to live one hundred years. A shorter line meant a shorter life. A person with the line ending half way was going to die at fifty. A break in line meant surviving a life-threatening event.

But this is not a "how to read palms" book. In the evening, when everyone was talking to each other and I was bored, I would take the palm of the cousin sitting nearest to me and tell him or her the future. Telling the future is not an exact science and it was key to say the right things. I had a natural skill in that area. Combining cousins' various tendencies, their expressed future goals, and their capabilities and desires, it was not hard to "tell the future" in such a way that made them think it was true.

Telling everyone stuff like "you are going to marry a very beautiful girl" or "you will be very successful in your career, but not as much as you should be" are axioms that no one can disagree with. For women, saying "the only person you care for in your life is your husband, but he does not appreciate your devotion" worked like magic.

The most important statements I learned, and used effectively, were the following:

- "You always try to help other people, but they do not reciprocate." Another variance: "You have a character fault: you always try to help people who do not care for you."
- "Everyone takes advantage of your good nature."
- To a person with a serious expression: "You will write a book that will change the world."

There is a lot of commonality between reading palms and lips. There is a lot of guesswork involved and the focus is not on the main target—lips or palms—but on the whole person. In lipreading, body language tells a lot and the same goes for palm reading. Both of these, in my opinion, are talents, not skills.

❖

For many deaf people, the ability to communicate with hearing people is important for their success. The less than 1 percent of the world population who are deaf do not provide a critical mass for a successful business venture. The ability to communicate effectively is essential to work as a professional in the huge hearing world. The number of deaf entrepreneurs successfully plying their trade within the deaf community is small. I am sure all of them would like to expand into the bigger world but for the communication hurdle.

A few years ago, the *Deaf Professional Network*, an e-magazine that was published for a couple of years, conducted a survey to find out the preferred mode of communication with their hearing coworkers. Some (16 percent) wrote back and forth and an equal number used keyboards and computers. The latter, after all, is a high-tech version of the former. What was surprising was that majority of respondents (65 percent) were divided equally (32 percent each) between those who used lipreading or used interpreters. The remaining 3 percent didn't communicate with hearing people. But then, perhaps they didn't communicate with deaf people, either.

Deaf people around the world are divided into two groups—those who can lipread and those who cannot. Superimposed on these two major groups are persons who can lipread but deny it and those who cannot lipread but claim they can. Thus, a simple communication skill, the ability to understand hearing people, has become a complicated issue that no one really discusses.

I am always amazed at how some deaf people can lipread. Growing up in a small village in the Himalayan foothills, lipreading to me was like America before 1492—it was there, but I did not know about it. There was no other deaf person in my village to compare notes with. People in my village would yell, stomp on the ground, flail their arms, and beat their brows to make me understand a simple sentence like "Are you deaf?" I have to be honest here and admit that I could lipread some words, but those were the kind of words my editor might edit out. Thus, my communication with hearing people was accomplished in writing, mostly with the index finger scrawling words on the palm.

Later in Delhi I met a deaf guy who was totally deaf like me but, to my great surprise, could lipread. He would look at a person speaking and then would speak back. I thought he was pulling a stunt. When I do not want to understand people or do not want them to know I am deaf, I also pull the same trick—appear to understand whatever nonsense they were uttering and smile in a very wise way and make some general response that would be analogous to "all of the above." This trick worked with the people who had just a passing interesting in me. But those who really wanted to discuss deep philosophical issues like, let us say, the weather, would catch on. Some telling me "It seems like it is going to rain today." might get a response like "You are right; it is going to be sunny today."

Lipreading, in my opinion, is neither science nor art; it is pure talent. Either you have it or you do not. Practice does not make perfect lipreaders or we would not have sign language. Practice, actually, only makes imperfect lipreaders, who specialize in misunderstanding everything. This practice has spawned a lot of deaf jokes that make us look like we have IQs three points below that of a brick.

A friend of mine who became deaf at the age of seventeen can lipread perfectly and people think she is not deaf. Believe me, she is amazing. She can lipread people with moustaches and those who barely move lips. I am sure she can lipread dead people in the dark. She is a genius in this area. I am on the farthest left side of bell curve.

Once, while visiting India, a businessman friend of mine had a meeting with a hearing businessman and he could not find an interpreter, mainly because there are no interpreters in Bombay. He cannot speak clearly but can lipread very well. He asked me to go along and we had a very successful meeting. He would sign and I would voice for him and then he would lipread the hearing man and sign to me. At the end of an hour, the hearing guy was ready to sign a contract. I do not know if it was the quality of the business proposal that my deaf friend had presented or our ingenuity and resourcefulness in developing a communication system. But I think it was his lipreading skill.

Unfortunately, my talent lay in the wrong area. Lipreading would have been much more beneficial to me.

❖

Back to Dan's palm!

I told him how old he would be when he was going to die, how many times he was going to marry, how many children he was going to have, what type of career he would take on, and the usual fare that goes with reading a palm. He was amused. To make it more interesting, I told him he had to depend heavily on his palm for sexual gratification. He laughed at that and knew I was bluffing all the time and trumped my last statement with his "researched" information that 92 percent of people used their palms and the remaining 8 percent lied. I knew I was trying to bullshit a bullshitter, but it was fun and we had a good laugh.

Then Dan became serious. He said we should go into business and charge something like fifty cents per read. I was only a few weeks in America and entrepreneurship was foreign to me. Also, I didn't feel comfortable being paid for telling lies. Fooling people for fun is OK, but being paid for them made it complicated. Dan was disappointed at my refusal but went along with it.

Dan, who rarely talked to people, suddenly became a very slick salesman. I do not know what he told and whom he told about my "expertise" palmistry, but the word was out. That evening someone knocked on our door, and when Dan opened it, there were about ten guys trying to get their heads in to take a look at me. Dan talked with them and had them line up against the wall in the hallway and then I started my palm reading. It took about two to three minutes to tell each person's fortune. The guy would look amazed at my knowledge of his future, stare at his palm trying to "read" it himself, and then leave as he was pushed outside by Dan and the person at the head of the line waiting for his turn.

This went on for a month. I am not sure how many palms I read, but I read plenty of them. Perhaps I had read the palms of all the students, as people stopped asking me. I had a pretty good memory for faces (not palms) and if someone tried to have his or her palm read a second time after a week, I would tell him or her I have already read it and could not read again. Actually, I was afraid that I might tell very different things during the second reading. Imagine having told a person that he will have two kids—one boy and one girl—and telling him that he was going to have four kids at the second reading!

I did read palms once in a while even after that but stopped totally during my junior year. I was eating breakfast in the cafeteria when a pretty girl joined me. She asked after sitting down if I remembered her. I didn't. She told me that I had read her palm two years earlier and had told her that she was going to drop out of college, marry, have a kid, and then return to college later.

"Do you know that everything you told me was correct? I got pregnant during my sophomore year here, left college, got married. My baby girl is over one year old now. She is with my mom. Now, here I am to finish college. How could you tell my future so accurately?" she asked.

How, indeed! I was dumbstruck and could not tell her anything. I didn't remember her, but I was sure that I had told her about dropping out and getting pregnant because I may have seen her playing around with boys all the time. What bothered me was that I might have unknowingly helped her follow a self-fulfilling prophecy route. I may have played a role in causing problems for her. What I was doing for fun had some grotesque results. I wondered how many others had believed me and lived the future I had foretold and hoped there were some good results. I never read palms after that morning.

9
Learning American English

THE BRITISH, ACCORDING TO AN INDIAN NATIONALIST leader, never left India. Their customs, dress, and, most of all, language has taken hold in India. English is not the national language of India, but de facto it is the language in which all official business is conducted. Since English is the key to a good job and advancement in life, every upward mobile young man strives to learn the language. I had decided to learn English after I became deaf. My experience in learning English was a major adventure.

I had learned English back in Gagret mostly on my own and surrounded by people who didn't speak English. I was proud of my command of English and people were amazed at how well I wrote. However, I was not prepared for "American" English and had a few problems after I started at Gallaudet.

The British or Indian spellings were not thought to be correct by Gallaudet students. In our French class, the teacher would ask us to write English translation of the French sentence she had given for homework. A fellow student looked at my writing and took me to the blackboard. Pointing to the word "colour," he erased "u" from it. I didn't say anything; I just shook my head in agreement even though I felt I was right and he was wrong. The other time, another student pointed to "learnt" that I had written on the board and changed it to "learned."

It was Terrence O'Rourke, my English teacher, who explained to me about my English. He took me to his office and wrote on paper. I still remember it verbatim: "You write well, and your grammar is correct. It is your British spelling and construction that are confusing. I suspect you have some influence of 'Indian English.'" This helped me understand why that student had "corrected" my spelling.

A month later, I needed a haircut and asked around where I could get one. Someone told me about a student who gave fifty-cent haircuts and who "was not really that bad a barber." I was led to a signup sheet posted in the Ely Hall lounge. This was another American invention for me. I had never seen sign-up sheets before but I liked this idea of communication.

I wrote my name on the sign-up sheet. The guy had written that he would cut hair in the first floor restroom of Ely Hall. The next day at the appointed time, I waited for my barber in the lounge. He didn't show up. After waiting for more than an hour, I thought maybe I was on the wrong floor. Therefore I asked a passing student pointing to the sign-up sheet where that "restroom" was. He told me to go straight ahead, turn right at the end of the corridor and the second door would be the restroom where this guy was giving haircuts. I followed directions and found myself in the bathroom. I didn't consider the student's trick very funny. I decided not to ask anyone again fearing the next guy might send me to another bathroom. At night, I asked Dan where the restroom was. He looked puzzled and asked, "Didn't you just come from there?" The light dawned upon me. "You mean a bathroom is called a restroom here?" I had thought that a restroom was where you rested—the drawing room— and that is why I was in the lounge, which in my opinion was the drawing room of our dormitory. How someone had decided to associate "resting" with the daily function of relieving oneself puzzled me and still does.

I learned more American English as I went along. Actually, I am still learning, as English, especially American English, is a dynamic language; it changes daily. All languages absorb new vocabularies as they come in contact with other languages and English in America perhaps has more contact with speakers of other languages that most other languages.

Of course, all foreign students were learning American English, but it was more problematic for me because of my habit of analyzing every word I learned. The need to decipher every new word or concept was part of habit. I could have formed it because a dictionary was not always available when I was reading and I would start trying to "invent" a meaning for the word by analyzing it. I still do that and come up with strange and wrong meanings of words and, especially, idioms.

All students complained about the cafeteria food. I thought it was OK, but my problem was the cafeteria didn't serve Indian food. I was a vegetarian and the overboiled vegetables that the cafeteria served were so bland that you have to be dying of hunger to eat them. The only meal

I enjoyed was the breakfast. The eggs, toast, and cereal along with juice and tea were great. Lunch and dinner were a problem and I ended up eating bread and butter during both meals.

I thought about living off campus and cooking my own meals even though I didn't know how to cook. A search on rentals in the *Washington Post* revealed rents to be much higher than dormitory rates. While doing research, I saw an advertisement for a "garage sale." An idea occurred to me that if I bought or leased a garage I would save some money and also cook on my own. I took the advertisement to the dormitory supervisor on duty and asked him to call the number and find out how much it would cost to rent a garage. He broke into a raucous laughter when he read the advertisement. I learned that they didn't sell garages at garage sales. The same goes for yards at yard sales.

The preposition gave me a lot of trouble. I had the habit of literally translating Hindi prepositions in English. But sitting on the table, I learned, means literally mounting the table; it has to be "at" instead. Then "up and down the street" referred to horizontal travel rather than vertical. Once in a very serious discussion, I suggested that we "must take the bull from its horns." The whole meeting broke out into a bawdy laughter. I sat there wondering why my very serious intent was being ridiculed.

My friend Kirk once brought a young lady friend by, who then took over the upkeep of the apartment we shared. She cleaned and cooked for us. I told Kirk, "Your girlfriend really is homely." He stared at me. "What makes you think that? She is beautiful."

"Yes," I agreed, "She is beautiful and also homely."

Kirk didn't agree with me.

An African friend went to a professional photographer to get a good photograph of himself since the counselor had told him to "present his best picture at the job interview." Then there were the succulent doughnuts that I fell in love with. My inquiries about the lack of nuts in them were met with ridicule. There were also some smiles, because, I learned later, the word "nuts" has other meanings too.

I had already learned that Americans played "football" with their hands (and no foul was called) and rarely touched it with a foot. The Americans do not live in their living rooms. When a boy and a girl took their car to "park" behind a building, they had some other purpose. They didn't put petrol in their car. Instead, they put in gas. I learned that gas was the same as petrol, and gas was short for gasoline.

As it happens, I am still learning American English and still make hilarious mistakes. But that is the fun of learning a language.

Then there were names for American events. I knew of Christmas but had never heard about Thanksgiving. Come November, when everyone began to talk about Thanksgiving, I was puzzled about who we were giving thanks to and for what. My queries resulted in various explanations about Indians and pilgrims, but due to my poor sign-reading skills and a total lack of American history, these explanations didn't make sense.

Before that came the "homecoming." Who was coming home and where was the home? Understanding and helpful students tried to explain to me much to their exasperation. They had grown up with the word and the idea that someone could not understand a term as simple as "homecoming" put them off. Later, St. Valentine's Day was another puzzle. It was interesting how many different explanations one can get. People do not like to appear dumb by just saying, "Sorry, I do not know the answer." Instead, they invent answers. I wish I had written down various explanations about Valentine's Day.

10

Learning Sign Language

MOST NEW STUDENTS WHO DIDN'T KNOW SIGN LANguage* were encouraged to come during the summer to learn sign language. Others learned some signs during the orientation period in the fall. However, I had arrived on the Friday before classes began, so I didn't have the opportunity to learn any signs. Without my knowledge, I was registered to attend a sign language class daily. I was so happy to have this class and was impressed how Gallaudet cared for its students.

There were eight of us in the class. The teacher, Norma, told us she was a junior. I could understand that, as I had learned that each fingertip stood for a class, touching the tip of the middle fingers sophomore and the index finger was junior. The thumb with its tip touching the center of the downward palm was senior. We looked in awe at Norma who was a full two years ahead of us. The thought my being a junior someday seemed like a major and lofty achievement far away in the obscure future.

My classmates were all new signers like me. Some of them had the benefit of summer sign training or orientation earlier in the month and could sign better than me. They were all friends and talked to each other whenever Norma's back was turned on us for writing something on the blackboard. I was surprised to see that all of them could talk and understand each other without signing. All of them were either hard of hearing or skilled lipreaders. I was neither.

However, I had the right attitude for learning signs and grasped each sign with eagerness as Norma taught us. The other students, especially one pretty girl with long, dark, wavy hair, would make a face at each sign and copy it as if she was doing it at gun point. She tried to talk to me and

---

* The term "American Sign Language" (ASL) was coined during the 1970s, so I am using the expression "sign language" as it was known and used at that time.

upon learning I didn't lipread, she signed-spelled slowly that she didn't need to learn signs. She could lipread, she could talk, she said. I didn't have the nerve to ask her why she came to Gallaudet if she didn't want to use signs. Soon I learned that this girl, whose name was Melanie, was not the only one who was not interested in signs and claimed to not need them. As time passed, however, they became fluent in signs and some of them later became sign language teachers.

One thing about our sign class intrigued me. Learning Indian signs was hard as it was an independent language. I had to forget my Hindi or English and focus on the Indian Sign Language, or ISL (the name that it got when it was first researched in 1977). In Norma's class, we used signs in English word order. We even talked while signing. In India, I could not do that. In "mixed" company of signers and nonsigners, I used to sign without voice and then speak so both groups could understand. Here at Gallaudet, they signed and spoke at the same time. It was interesting and made it easier for people like me who knew English. Thus, I focused on sign vocabulary.

I did notice that some of Gallaudet students didn't use English word order while signing to each other. Actually, most of them followed this non-English grammar format. I didn't understand them, but I attributed that to my inability to read signs at normal speed. I did ask one guy about signing in non-English word order and he just shook his head.

"They are low verbal students," he explained.

"Meaning?"

"They do not know enough English; therefore they use broken English," he explained further.

I wondered how "low verbal" or "broken English" students could get into a college. It took me a while to learn more about this phenomenon. At that time, I was glad that American signs were in English word order. The practice of signing and speaking at the same time also fascinated me. I wrote to Suraj, a deaf associate in India, explaining how Americans have developed this system known as Simultaneous Communication (SimCom) and how we need to develop similar "advanced" methods in India. Suraj was impressed and said they will have to wait until I return, so I could demonstrate this system in person and help pave the way for its development in India.

A month or so later, Norma told me that I didn't need the class anymore. I was upset because I didn't feel my signing ability was up to par yet. But she meant that I was able to follow professors in the classroom and I could understand other students in the dining room. But Norma said I knew all the signs in the book we used and I had to practice reading signs on my own. This meant reading more palms—I read Norma's palm also.

It took me almost a year before I was able to understand the teacher in classrooms fully and participate in discussion with other students without the "What did you say?" or "Will you please repeat?" requests. I also began to pick up some signs that didn't have English equivalents and also signs that had many English meanings. For example, thumb and index finger joined like 'O' touching the upper part of the chin, just below the lips, can mean "expert" or "daredevil" and more. That made me wonder at times about signing and speaking at the same time. Sign language, I began to understand, was a different language and not just a vehicle to visually represent English.

11

Being Alone in a Crowd

IN INDIA, PEOPLE SAY "NAMASTE" WITH BOTH PALMS clasped together in front of you when they meet each other. Friends just shake hands, a relic of British times, which Indian people use a lot more than the British. "Namaste" is a more formal greeting. We greeted our boss with a "Good morning, sir." Each morning, Indian people shake hands with friends and all their fellow employees and again when they take their leave.

Each morning, while going for breakfast to the cafeteria with books and notebooks tucked under my left arm, I would approach everyone I knew and shake his or her hand. When I arrived in the classroom, I would shake hands of classmates who were friendly. Why they would smile at my handshaking puzzled me a bit, but I didn't pay attention to it.

One morning, I stopped to shake hands with Zug, a short, friendly guy, and he, in a tired manner, didn't offer his hand.

"Why do you shake hands every day?" he asked.

I could not answer him. His question was analogous to "Why are you friendly?" or even "Why do you breathe?" He shifted from one foot to another, as if he had an uncomfortable duty to perform, and finally said, "Look, some of us were talking about your shaking hands daily and are tired of it. We shake hands only when we meet people after a long time. OK?"

It was really embarrassing to know that for the last several weeks, they were laughing behind my back at the "weird habits of that Indian guy." I pulled my hand back, awkwardly put it in my pocket, and walked away. There were no more daily handshakings in my morning greetings.

The Americans, I learned, had a number of forms of greetings. Some spelled a quick "hi" and others waved. Mr. Phillips, the dean of students, always winked when he passed me. A wink in India is a clear message of sexual interest; therefore, I didn't wink back. It did disconcert me a bit, so I asked Dan and he just laughed. The wink was just another form of "hi" in America.

Then, there was the hug. Boys and girls hugged each other when they passed each other on the sidewalk, in the cafeteria, or in the lounge. First I thought, they hugged their girl- or boyfriend, but then I noticed a boy hugging several girls in a line. It was another form of greeting. In India, the closest you came to girl you knew was a yard. Any closer, you got slapped for being "fresh." It took me a long time to get used to this "greeting," as nice as it is. I didn't notice that boys didn't hug boys. However, that is a story unto itself.

I told one guy who was interested in Hindi language that the word "hi" also means "ouch." After that, every time he passed me, he would spell o-u-c-h in greeting. No more Hindi meanings of English words for him or anyone, I decided.

In Delhi, I was used to being the center of attention or at least was recognized. It was fun working in the National Physical Laboratory where, despite my being the only deaf person, I got along very well with my coworkers. At the All India Federation of the Deaf and the Delhi Association of the Deaf, I was considered a leader and was used to people coming to me and trying to get my attention.

No one knew me at Gallaudet. I felt like a persona non grata. I longed for my old friends and thought of the long discussions I used to have with them and the laughs we all shared. I didn't have a single friend here. There were some like Godsey who, after saying hi, stopped by to chat a bit. Dan was friendly at times but kept his distance. My efforts to make friends were a total failure mostly due to my shaky command of American signs and a nagging lack of interest on most students' part.

After meals and between classes, I would look at the small or large groups of students talking animatedly with each other and laughing. Of course, I could not follow their conversations and could not really look at the people I didn't know for long. The loneliness was intensified by the fact that there were over one thousand students at Gallaudet. They were around me, in my classes, in the dormitories, but they were not with me. They passed me, talking to each other; they smiled politely at my efforts to talk to them and looked relieved when I gave up. Some were even more direct with a curt "I am busy" or the more diplomatic "I am supposed to be working on something" and walked away leaving me signing to myself.

I felt invisible. The one-thousand-plus students at Gallaudet didn't see me. It felt like I was back in the fields of Gagret herding cows by myself. This feeling of being lonely in a crowded college made me feel depressed, and I longed to go back to Delhi, at least for the weekends. However, I knew I would not be able to afford to visit India for six years. The cost of a roundtrip ticket was prohibitive. It cost about $1,000 at that time. It would have taken me years to save that much money.

However, I consoled myself by remembering my initial meetings with deaf people in Delhi back in 1961. They had ignored me because of my then-limited signing ability and because I was from a village. My efforts to become friendly with most of them were sneered at. I had given up making friends until I had Kesh and others who became close friends. It had taken several months before I was "recognized" in Delhi. I will, I told myself, make friends here too. I also hoped that I would become a leader as well, even a minor one since everyone here was a college student.

12

Cultural Abyss

HAVING READ BOOKS BY ZANE GRAY, EDNA FERBER, EARL Stanley Gardner, and some other American writers, I felt that I knew American culture pretty well and didn't expect any cultural problems. I knew how Americans dressed, what they ate, how they behaved, and what the general customs were. However, I learned the hard way that my knowledge about American culture was sketchy or erratic. Some experiences were funny and some embarrassing. I can look back and laugh at those experiences now, but they were not very funny then, either for me or for others involved.

The Sunday *Washington Post* was a joy. It had more pages than an Indian newspaper's combined issues for one month. The comics alone were a dozen pages. Of course, most of the paper was devoted to advertising things I could not afford.

Most students slept in late on weekends, but being a morning person, I usually woke up at six or seven in the morning, even on weekends. I came down to the lounge wearing my pajamas and slippers, got the hefty newspaper, and sat down on a sofa to read it.

Just before I had finished reading the main section, a student passed me. I said hi to him. He didn't respond, just walked on hurriedly and then came back. He gave me head to toe inspection like a mother does before sending a child to school and shook his head.

"You know that girls will be coming here soon." He kept looking up and down while making this important announcement.

"Nice." I smiled.

"You need to change clothes before they come." He was very serious.

"Why?" I was puzzled.

We went back and forth and I learned that I was not supposed to come out of our room in my pajamas. That didn't make sense to me. My body was covered from neck to toe in my pajamas. The guy who was faulting my dress code had no shirt and was wearing a tattered shorts that he had designed by cutting off his jeans. The idea that I should change my pajamas to cut off jeans to be presentable to the visiting girls just was too difficult for me to grasp.

"You think you are dressed properly?" A rhetorical question from me.

He didn't dignify my question by responding to it. I got up and went upstairs to wear my suit.

In Gagret, we didn't have special sleeping suits or pajamas. What we wore all day was what we slept in. In Delhi, we used pajamas or other loose shirts for sleeping. But that ensemble was fine for going out for a walk in the morning or going to the bazaar. Going out in a pair of skimpy shorts and without a shirt is not considered appropriate for a grown-up man.

An American girl can go to the beach in a thong bikini, which shows 99 percent of her breasts and barely hides her private areas, but she cannot go to the beach in her pajamas or a nightgown.

Another dress gaffe I made was when I used my *chappals* or sandals with my suit and tie for dinner in the cafeteria. During the fall of 1967, the Hot Shoppe people who ran the cafeteria decided to have "family-style" dinners. We had to dress up and sit as a family while some of the hired students served food to us. Everyone hated it, but you had a choice to go hungry, eat out, or wear a suit or dress. I didn't mind wearing a suit, as I did it even for attending classes. Following my Indian habits, I used sandals with the suit. I became aware while standing in the line for the cafeteria to open that some of the students were looking at my sandals furtively and talking to each other. Finally, one of them came over to me and very politely asked me, "Please go back to your room and put on proper shoes." I looked at their shoes. They all wore pump shoes or tasseled dress shoes. No one, except for the girls, wore sandals. As I look back, my old Indian sandals under the really neat suit must have looked gross to my fellow students. But at that time, I didn't see anything wrong with my clothes.

Despite the student's repeated requests, I refused to go change and told him that the announcement we had received about family-style dining only suggested that men wear suits and women wear dresses. There was no mention of shoes or sandals. He gave up but was not very happy about it. Nor were other students who finally stopped looking at me.

Americans love privacy. They do not share much about themselves. In India, almost everything one does is like an open book. For example, if one sees a friend wearing a new shirt, it is OK to ask, "Where did you buy it and how much did you pay for it?" It is also OK to ask, "What is your salary?" or "How much money have you saved up?" Even "Are you happy with your wife?" is a question that reflects your concern about the individual.

At Gallaudet, my polite inquiries about their personal affairs generated shock and annoyance. The nicest response to my questions was "None of your business." They also interjected some words before the word "business." I acquired a pretty good vocabulary of four-letter words while checking on my new friends' general welfare.

When someone sitting at the same table for a meal would leave, he or she would make a big deal of their departure with the "excuse me." Now, I didn't understand what mistake they had made that required my excusing them. These students have grown up in a culture where they were taught to excuse themselves when they left the dining table or a meeting. They must have thought that I was really rude since I didn't excuse myself when I picked up my tray or left a group. I did, however, say "excuse me" or "sorry" if I bumped into someone accidentally.

The same goes for thanking people for passing the bread or doing minor thing. In India you do not thank or apologize to someone unless you really are thankful or are sorry. The continuing "thank you" baffled me. I must have been thought to be very rude since I only thanked people when I really meant it and not just for passing the potato dish to me.

In India, two male friends or cousins can touch each other freely. They walk hand-in-hand and friends and relatives hug each other when meeting for the first time in a while. This is basically the same as American women, who hug each other, walk with arms around one another, and hold hands. I was not aware of the American phobia of touching other men. In the 1960s, men touched each other only when shaking hands or patting backs.

At Gallaudet, I touched other boys like I did in India. I realized it was unacceptable one day in the cafeteria. After dinner, I was sitting and talking with a new friend at an empty table. I had, without being aware of it, placed my hand on my friend's forearm. We had been laughing at something when he suddenly slapped me on my wrist and pushed my hand away.

"QUEER!" He spelled, his face distorted in disgust.

The word "queer" to me meant "strange." What strange thing did I do? Did it have something to do with placing my hand on his arm for longer than two seconds? Shocked and also insulted, I left the table and went to my room. I had lost a friend I enjoyed talking to and friends at that time were in short supply.

I asked Dan, my unofficial tutor for culture and other things American, what queer in America meant. He asked me first to explain the whole situation. At the end of my story, he asked, "Do you mean, you had your hand on his arm like a boy would put on a girl?'

"No," I retorted, "like a boy would put on a boy. Nothing wrong with it."

Dan appeared exasperated. Slowly, he explained that only homosexuals or "queers" touched other boys. He knew I was married and I must have not given him any indication of being "queer," so he didn't question my sexual orientation. He did, however, advise me to keep my hands to myself. This kind of advice is given in India in the context of girls. Boys do not touch girls, not in public anyway. In America, one didn't touch boys in the 1960s.

But the girls did touch boys and vice versa. The public demonstrations of affection embarrassed me. My first experience was when Dan and I were going to the infirmary to get some aspirin for Dan's headache. As we came out of the side door of Ely Hall, I froze in my tracks. A girl was standing on the ground with her upper torso inside the window of the dormitory room. She was necking with the boy inside the window. The boy's hands were very busy. Dan had walked ahead. He returned and saw the whole scene: a boy and a girl involved in heavy petting and me standing there ogling them. He told me to come and stop being a voyeur. I pointed at the couple and said, "Look, they are doing it in public like cats and dogs."

Dan told me to hurry up and move. Seeing his urgency, I followed him while backing slowly and looking at the spectacle. Dan warned me that it was not nice to ogle at lovers in action. The boy might get angry and teach me a lesson in good manners.

I had to accept that these public demonstrations of affection and other things were acceptable in America. In India, where even holding hands during that time was considered offensive, such acts could be punished

by jail. Usually, the well-meaning or rather jealous citizens became vigi-
lantes and taught a lesson to the offending lovers.

These were some of my first experiences in America. There was never
a day when I didn't learn a new thing. Some of them were funny, some
crude, and some totally embarrassing. However, within a year, I was at
home at Gallaudet. I made friends, learned sign language, took classes,
and joined the mainstream of the Gallaudet community.

13

Back to Photography

ALL MY EDUCATIONAL EXPENSES AT GALLAUDET WERE paid for by a grant-in-aid. The only expenses I had were books, clothes, and cigarettes. I had sworn off smoking when I left India and had vowed to lead a real spartan life like Gandhi did. However, Dan had a carton of cigarettes and had told me help myself. I had decided to take one cigarette to get an idea what an American cigarette tastes like. That was the famous last word, or rather, the famous last cigarette. I was hooked again and Dan's carton was gone in no time. He didn't have any money to buy another carton, so I had to dig out of my meager supply of dollars to buy my "last packet" of cigarettes. And that cost 35 cents in the vending machine.

I remember the photography place where they took the mug shots for identity cards and also remembered the fancy cameras they had. The idea of getting my hands on a sparkling new Nikon, which I had seen only in advertisements or from a distance, was tempting enough for me to earn some money. This helped me overcome my fear and go visit the place in the basement of the old counseling center. The supervisor of the photography department was sitting and talking to another guy there when I entered the room. I was thinking about my first interview for a photography job three years earlier and was nervous like a beggar. I was going to beg for a job that they had not advertised.

Frank, the supervisor, looked at me. I forgot that Americans didn't understand my Gagret-accented English and asked, "Do you need a photographer?" Frank understood me, however. He began to speak and when I shook my head, he took out his pen and began to write. He wrote in large capital letters. He wrote and I spoke, wondering how he could understand me or if he really did. Ten minutes later, I walked out with my feet about one foot in the air. I had a job offer working twenty hours a week at $1.25

an hour. That was, I figured as I walked back to Ely Hall, about eleven rupees an hour. I was going to earn working part-time in one week as much as I earned working for a whole month full-time in India.

Then there was the interview. The only question Frank had asked me was if I knew how to develop photos. My mere mention of the fact that I had worked professionally for six years closed the interview. He didn't ask me, "You are deaf. How will you be able to work?" He didn't make me stand in the middle of the room but had offered a chair next to him. He told me to bring my class schedule and we could work out a schedule together. He also instructed me to keep record of all the time I worked for payment later. As I was leaving he shook my hand. This was a little unnerving. Bosses didn't shake the hands of their underlings in India.

I started working the next day. There was a Student Body Government (SBG) meeting and I was to take a few photographs of officers and participating students. I was wondering about the camera when he took me to a cupboard and pointed at the three 35-mm single lens reflex cameras and an array of lenses sitting there. I picked a Minolta, two lenses, and a flashgun. Frank told me to take these with me to the dorm as the student meeting was in the evening. Walking with the expensive camera and spare lenses, holding them like a baby, I felt like a king.

It took me fifteen minutes to shoot the SBG meeting. After classes the next day, I took the photographic equipment and went to the darkroom. I told Frank that I had used only ten shots and there were twenty-six more shots left on the film. If he needed photos now, I could cut the film and develop it for printing.

"What do you mean by cutting the film?" Frank asked.

"I will cut the used film and develop it and save the rest for future shootings." I explained.

"NO, NO!" He wrote on a sheet of paper, "YOU DEVELOP THE WHOLE FILM. WE DO NOT NEED TO CUT IT."

Film is expensive and developing the unexposed film would have been a great waste. In India, I had developed whatever was shot and saved the film. Here, such practice was unthinkable. I didn't feel comfortable, but then I thought about the number of glasses of milk and the huge amount of food that was thrown in the cafeteria sink daily and want to the darkroom and began to load the film on a spool for developing.

After developing the film, I asked Frank where I could store the developer. He casually pointed to the sink. More waste. I dried the film and made several prints as instructed by Frank. I took them to Frank after trimming them. He looked at them carefully and pointed at some white spots on two prints caused by dust specks on the negatives. I was embarrassed and braced myself for a lecture and apologized to him. I told him that I would retouch them if he would show me where the retouching brush and ink was.

He didn't rebuke me and told me there was no retouching equipment. He took the two prints, tore them, and threw them in the wastebasket. Then he hunted for a small brush for cleaning negatives, cleaned them, and asked me to print the two photos again. I went back to the darkroom and began to compare the difference between Indian and American bosses. He had expected me to make mistakes and help me. In India, in a similar situation, the boss would have chastised the worker telling him about his intelligence level and that of his parents and grandparents. In between this analysis, he would have also established very close intimacy with the worker's sisters and mother.

Frank gave me a timecard and I filled out fifteen minutes for taking the photographs and an hour for developing and printing it. I didn't enter the time I used for reprinting the defective prints. He didn't look at the card and put it in a slot on his desk telling me to fill out my time on a daily basis.

The next day I went back again and asked Frank if there was any work for me. He looked around and then had an idea. After checking with Jim, the other guy working in the photography department, he found some negatives and asked me to make five-by-seven-inch prints of them. To impress him, I worked fast and finished printing in a few minutes, then washed, dried, and trimmed the prints. It took me an hour and after giving the prints to Frank, I put down one hour on my card. He looked at the card and then sighed, scratched his head, asked me to take a seat, and began to consult with Jim.

I wondered what I did wrong. I was sure I was totally honest with my time and prepared myself to defend my claim if he wanted to undercut me. After five or so minutes of discussions, Frank began to work on a sheet of paper. Then he showed it to Jim and then Jim began to sign to me haltingly.

Frank had changed my fifteen minutes for taking photographs at the SBG meeting to one hour. Jim told me that I have to charge time "from door to door," a new expression for me. I understood that I had to count my time from the point when I left the dormitory room to returning there after the assignment. He also changed the time I had spent in the darkroom by adding the time I had decided not to charge for my mistake. At the end of our discussions, I had more than twice the time I had entered. I thanked both Frank and Jim and went to the cafeteria, elated at the huge amount of money I was making for not working.

This job in the photography department lasted me the whole six years while I was a student at Gallaudet. Frank knew very little about photography and was happy to have me there. He didn't want to stay late to shoot photographers, either. This was a perfect work for me. There was a lot of flexibility of time and I didn't have to travel off campus.

They added two full-time photographers over the years, but there was always enough work for me to fill up the twenty hours a week quota. My job changed and I got more responsibilities. One of them was filming all football games on a super-8 movie camera. Later, I began to videotape those games using "portable" videotaping equipment that weighed about forty pounds.

During the summer, I worked full-time. Gallaudet offered free room and access to a kitchen on campus. This helped me earn enough money for books, clothes, and other personal items. I also saved money for helping with my tuition.

14

The Missing Bag

YOU MIGHT BE WONDERING WHAT HAPPENED TO THE bag that TWA had lost. Every day I would ask the dormitory supervisor to call the number the nice lady at the Dulles airport had given me. We would go through all the details—flight number, dates, ticket number—and learn they didn't know where the bag was and it would show up soon and I should call the next day. This continued for almost a month.

Meanwhile, I had to find a way to survive while waiting for the suitcase to arrive. Fortunately, I had two changes of clothes and toiletries with me. These were in my carry-on bag put there as there was not enough space in the bag I had checked in. Dan, on seeing my meager belongings, would ask if my trunk had arrived. It seemed all students had arrived at Gallaudet with a trunk and not with a bag. I decided not to be any different and started using the word "trunk" to describe my missing suitcase.

I was not aware that the airline was supposed to give me some kind of money to purchase clothes and other necessities. The airline personnel didn't offer any help, either. So the only alternative was to wash clothes every three or four days. Dan helped with that by taking me to the basement of Ely Hall and teaching me how to use the washer and dryer. He also loaned me his iron. Thus, I was able to survive on my two pairs of clothes for the whole month.

Finally, the famous bag arrived in late October. Dan was disappointed when he saw my "trunk" and asked where the trunk was I had been talking about. I was embarrassed and remained quiet.

I opened my suitcase, which had just three more pairs of clothes, another suit, and some gifts for "American benefactors" that Narain insisted I take. Narain had suggested giving these gifts to whoever I felt helped me. However, I never could decide on what to give whom. Later, Dan and I used those ourselves. Dan watched me unpack my meager worldly possessions. After I had emptied the suitcase, half the drawers in my chest were still empty. By American standards my possessions were bare bones. The missing "trunk" had arrived and I was glad that I had all my things. To Dan, these must have looked like what an American packs for a weekend trip. However, he didn't say anything.

On a rack in my basement, a tattered beige suitcase sits empty. This suitcase has traveled, empty, with my family to Maryland, Texas, Illinois, North Carolina, New Mexico, and finally to Virginia, a few miles from the Dulles airport where it had arrived first. It looks small, very small. It is hard for me to imagine that I had two suits, three pairs of clothes, and other stuff packed in it to start my life in America. I do not have anything from September 13, 1967, when I came to America left with me, except this suitcase.

15
Progress in Classes

AS I LEARNED SIGNS AND GOT THE HANG OF THE AMERI-can educational system, I felt more comfortable. Being a student after sixteen years of farm and photography work was not easy in the beginning. In India, all school terms, including colleges, had one full year. At Gallaudet, the year was divided into two semesters, which confused me. The grading system was also confusing. Opposed to the Indian percent system, Americans used letter grades. These letter grades, as I learned more about them, didn't measure accurately. For example, if someone scored 89 percent, that person would get a B and another person with 90 percent would get an A. Thus, a score of one percent could kick one up by 9 percent. Later, as I earned grades, I found that teachers, being human, rarely gave a B if someone had scored 89 or even 88 percent.

I liked the quick and periodic testing. Indian schools held a final examination at the end of the year to measure the whole year's learning. In American universities, they have tests and quizzes, which is easier on students. Then, at the end of the semester, you were ready for the second semester with new courses. I was so relieved to learn that the semesters were independent of each other.

I was worried about failing. Gallaudet was the world's only college for the deaf, and American education was supposed to be harder than Indian education. That's what I was told. The thought of failing and being kicked out of the college was scary. Imagine my going back to India at the end of the semester after failing. Everyone would have laughed and I would have no job as the photography job I had was not there for the taking.

This fear was a great motivator. I never cut class and never missed doing homework. As the semester progressed, students began to talk about two new terms: academic probation (AP) and academic dismissal (AD). What did these mean? I asked around and was told that scoring less than 60 percent on midterm examinations or getting all Ds would result in academic probation, and getting some Fs in addition would result in an automatic AD and expulsion. I decided that I was not going to get that.

At the end of the first semester, I managed to score over 87 percent and made the dean's list, or DL, as it is generally known. I felt relieved. I had scored higher than 95 percent of the students in my class despite working twenty hours a week as a photographer and reading a lot of books for pleasure.

There were students who had transferred from "hearing" universities, including Dan, who claimed that Gallaudet was a "high school." I had not attended a high school either here or in India, so could not give my opinion about the academic rigor at Gallaudet during my time. However, I had to admit that getting on the DL was not that hard at Gallaudet. Since only a small number of students made the DL, I wondered what the other students did most of the time. They had no jobs and were full-time students. This made me wonder about their motivation or the lack thereof. Except for a small number of students, most did not seem to be much interested in going to classes. Sports and social life took the front seat to studies.

Despite the easy coursework, almost a hundred students managed to get AD at the end of the year. These students spent their time lounging around talking, watching television, and going off campus to drink. These students managed to show up after a year or so. Some of them, having learned a lesson, woke up and managed to graduate after five or six years at Gallaudet. Some never did but kept coming back to Gallaudet mostly for the rich social life Gallaudet offered.

Almost all students had what they called vocational rehabilitation, or VR, support. This support included tuition, fees, room, board, and books. This support differed from state to state. For example, California paid very generously and even paid its students' roundtrip fare to attend Gallaudet. Actually, the state chartered a plane to bring all students. The allowance for books was very generous too. One Californian student upon learning that I paid for books myself, made a deal with me. He would charge my books to his state VR account and I would pay 50 percent of the price to him in cash. This was not very kosher, but I told myself I was just getting some support from the California VR.

16

The First Thanksgiving

STUDENTS AND TEACHERS BEGAN TO TALK ABOUT A MYS-
terious event called "Thanksgiving" around November. Many were going
to their homes and had invited their friends whose homes were too far
for travel. Some students asked me if I was going home for Thanksgiving.
These were either naïve inquiries or mocking comments. I knew I would
not be able to afford to visit my family until I had finished my studies and
that was going to take six long years.

Lulu, a student from Hong Kong, stopped in the hallway and asked
if I would like to go to Williamsburg for Thanksgiving. I told her "no"
right away as I had no money and didn't know where Williamsburg was
and why anyone would want to go to Williamsburg for Thanksgiving.
She left but met me again after the class and slowly explained that it
would not cost me a penny and that three people were going—she, a
Canadian girl, and myself. I asked her who was paying for travel, hotel,
and food. She responded that an English teacher who is an active member
of the Baptist church was going to drive us and that the Baptist church
was going to take care of all expenses.

The only Christian churches I knew were Catholic and Protestant.
This Baptist church was a new thing for me. I wondered what it was and
whether they were trying to make me a Christian. She read my face and
said that she was a Buddhist and was not going to become a Christian.
The Canadian girl was her roommate and friend and had assured her that
the trip was not going to be an attempt to convert us. I told her I would
let her know later.

The only person who could advise me on such a matter was Dan. He
thought it would be good for me to go visit Williamsburg and Jamestown
and explained that these places were the sites of some of the first colonies in America back in 1607. I liked history and the idea of seeing stuff

from 1607 America pushed the Baptist part to the background. I found Lulu and told her that I would go. She told me that Miss Polly Shahan, the teacher, was going to pick us up the next day, Thursday, at eight in the morning.

The campus was deserted that Wednesday by noon. Dan and I decided to do some exploring. We walked from Gallaudet to the Washington Monument with Dan leading the way. He didn't need a map or directions from anyone, I noticed. He used the grid-like layout of the city and walked from 4th to 5th Streets to reach 17th Street where the Washington Monument is.

We both must have made a funny pair. Dan, thin and tall, quiet and All American and me short, dark, and trying to smile, even at trees. We didn't talk. Dan talked when he was in the mood. Other times, he remained silent. I was used to his moods and got myself into the "silent" mood.

We rode the elevator to its top for a nice view of the city. I wondered how they had managed to put the elevator in it. The Qutab Minar in Delhi, the world's tallest brick minaret built in the thirteenth century, is only one-third the height of the Washington Monument and climbing its three hundred stairs is very difficult. How did people climb the eight hundred stairs of the Washington Monument before they put in the elevator? How did they carry huge blocks of rock while they were creating it? Then I thought about the Qutab Minar, which was built about five hundred years before the Washington Monument. All of this work was done before they invented cranes and before electricity made it possible for us to ride all the way up without lifting a leg.

Later, we walked to Georgetown. We had been on the road for more than two hours and it was a bit chilly. I needed to use the bathroom. Dan said there was no bathroom around here and I would have to be patient until we reached Georgetown. I was surprised at this lack of bathroom amenities in America. Indian cities have urinals every other block. If not, people stopped at a wall to relieve themselves. I asked Dan why they didn't have bathrooms on each block. He didn't like my question and told me that people here travel in cars and do not walk like us. Gas stations, he added, had bathrooms. There were no gas stations around the Washington monument; therefore there was no bathroom. Actually, there was one. An old stone building, which might have been built around the same time as the monument was, was converted into a bathroom. Dan had to ask a few people before we were pointed to it.

Finally, we arrived in Georgetown. We were tired and thirsty. Dan suggested we stop for a beer. We went into a small restaurant on Wisconsin Avenue and established ourselves in a bay window. We drank beer and watched people hurrying back and forth on the sidewalks. Everyone was in a big hurry. I wondered if they were late for catching a train. Why was everyone hurrying? Why wasn't even one person walking leisurely like us? Later, as time passed, I learned that hurrying was a habit. However, by the time I learned about it, I had developed that habit myself. I watched the rushing people and enjoyed my first beer in America.

The next morning, I packed my small attaché case with clothes and went to the parking lot outside the Hall Memorial Building as I had been instructed to do by Lulu. Lulu and Charmaine, the Canadian student, were already there. They were good friends and roommates and were talking animatedly about something. They forget I was there after saying "hi." I stood there wondering if I should go back to my room because spending three days being ignored was not my idea of fun. At that time, a car drove up and a white-haired woman jumped out of it. She was a bit plump but very quick on her feet. She came to me with her hand extended and asked the girls to introduce me to her. Lulu came forward and introduced me to Miss Shahan by saying, "This is Madan from India with a very long funny name." Miss Shahan asked me to spell my last name and tried to copy it from memory and failed. However, she managed to spell it perfectly after her third attempt.

We put our bags in the trunk of her car. I sat in front with Miss Shahan and the two friends took over the backseat, where they continued to talk nonstop. I sat there erect and wished I had brought a book. However, soon after we left the city, I no longer wanted a book. The cars, the road, and the passing scenery captivated me. It was all very different from what I had seen in my life.

The first thing that puzzled or fascinated me was a total lack of traffic lights or people walking beside the road. I didn't expect cows and dogs like we have in India. I did, however, expect people around the road. There were none. Our car joined other cars driving more than seventy miles per hour. I noticed the green speed limit signs and also took a quick look at the speedometer of our car. Miss Shahan was a fastidious driver. She kept the needle at seventy most of the time. Other cars passed her driving pretty quickly. I guessed they were doing eighty or ninety miles per hour and wished Miss Shahan drove faster.

We drove for almost four hours with a short stop at a rest area. The endless rolling hills with green grass and green trees amazed me. We did pass some small towns, but they were just a blur. The trees and the beautiful landscape dominated the passing scenery. I looked at the people inside the cars that passed us. There were usually one or two persons in one car. There were station wagons with whole families also. But no car had more than three or four passengers. In India, a car was usually packed with four people. At times, six or more people managed to squeeze in one small car. It must be nice, I thought, to have all of this space to yourself in the car. At the same time, I wondered if these people could share cars and save gas. But saving seemed like the last thing the Americans thought about.

We arrived in Williamsburg around noon. Miss Shahan led our little caravan carrying our small bags to the hotel lobby where she gave the clerk our names. She kept signing all the time while talking to the clerk. I could follow the exchange most of the time. This was an interesting experience. Why was she signing to the hearing man? Lulu and Charmaine didn't even pay attention to all of this as they were still busy talking. Those two girls could really talk. I noticed Miss Shahan had memorized my name, and I was impressed with her diligence.

After registration, Miss Shahan gave me one key and told me to go the room number written on the ring. She explained that all men were staying in one wing and the women in the other wing. Both Lulu and Charmaine giggled at this. I didn't know what was funny about the men having a separate wing. Miss Shahan asked me to meet everyone in thirty minutes in the lobby so we could go to lunch.

I took the key and my attaché case and found the room assigned to me. Upon entering, I saw four beds cramped in a small room. There was less than six inches of space between each bed. Sprawled on the three beds were three young African men. They were looking at me as I entered and smiled in unison. I smiled back and touched my ear and shook my head when I saw them talking to me. They shook their heads and each of them rose from bed to shake my hand and say something. I asked them to please write, at which point one of the guys found a notebook and wrote down their names. I asked if they were friends. They shook their heads. Just like me, they were assigned to this room. They were students from other universities and had come here, like me, as guests for Thanksgiving.

I went back to the lobby after placing my attaché case on the empty bed and waited for the ladies to return. Now I understood that this special gathering was for foreign students like Lulu, Charmaine, my African roommates, and me. I wondered how many more students were there.

At lunch, I found the answer. There were about seventy foreign students and about forty American students who helped the hosts. We had a nice lunch with a short welcome speech by a young man. Miss Shahan interpreted every word he said. She introduced us to people and kept signing all the time. I was impressed with her energy and strong desire to please everyone. She smiled at everyone and shook hands with some people she had met before. She introduced us to her acquaintants and interpreted their questions and voiced our answers to them. This went on during the whole lunch.

We were each given name tags and a program booklet at a registration table. I looked at the schedule; it was full for three days. Every hour except for the sleeping time was covered. We had several meetings and sightseeing tours to Williamsburg and Jamestown. We had to attend plays and lectures. All of this was to end on Sunday morning and it was just Thursday. We visited the old fort in Jamestown and all the well-preserved buildings in Williamsburg. There were nonstop commentaries by the guides dressed in what I later learned to be colonial-era clothes. Our teacher interpreted nonstop even when we were not paying attention to her.

I learned a lot about American history during the next three days. I didn't learn anything about Christian religion, however. The main problem was Miss Shanahan's signing speed. She signed at normal level, which was too fast for me. I only got half of what she signed and, lacking the context, that half didn't make much sense to me. Thus, I sat in various meetings, breakfast, lunch, and dinner speeches for the next three days without really understanding anything. Visiting the sites was different. There were brochures and signs everywhere. These with some interpreted information from Miss Shahan helped me get a pretty good grasp of how colonies began in America.

The hotel was not bad and the food was pretty good. I ate my first turkey and they served chicken once. The breakfast with eggs and hash brown potatoes was always my favorite meal. When they served ham or beef, I ate vegetables and bread with butter. I would put on a lot of black pepper to make my vegetables "interesting."

The only painful part of the stay was answering questions from Lulu. She had developed an intense dislike for me for some reason. She made comments about my pepper on vegetables and asked why I didn't eat meat, adding "because you Hindus think cows are sacred," with a sardonic laugh. Charmaine was nice. She didn't ask any questions to make fun of me but didn't stop Lulu from asking, either. Miss Shahan did catch some of these questions but just smiled. She didn't scold us, either.

We had socials after lunch and dinner. Most of the American students socialized with the foreign students. We three deaf students were left alone after they exchanged greetings with us. None of them knew signs or were interested in learning. However, one brave young woman named Diane became friendly with me. She got paper and a pen and started asking questions about India and Gallaudet. I answered in writing as she didn't understand my speech. Pretty soon we had become friends and filled out quite a few sheets of her notebook. She was from a city called Roanoke. I asked where this Roanoke was. "Just a couple of hours' drive from here," she explained. Americans do not measure distance with miles or kilometers, they measure it with hours. I guessed Roanoke was 140 miles from Williamsburg.

My exchange with Diane gave Lulu more fodder to pick on me.

"You told us you are married. Why are you flirting with that girl?" she asked with a smirk.

"I am not flirting with her. We are just discussing cultural differences between India and the United States." I was irritated.

"You mean India has culture!" Lulu laughed. She was a hoot to herself. I kept smiling while I wished she could go away.

On the second day, Miss Shahan announced that we were going to sing something in signs for the whole group. She passed out sheets of paper to us three to read and memorize the song. It had a funny ending: "kumbaya." I didn't know what "kumbaya" meant, until Miss Shahan translated it into signs "come here." It was fun practicing the song. If it was a Christian song, that was fine with me. Basically, all religions ask God, gods, or the Lord to come help us. Since Hindu religion has taught me to respect all religions equally, I didn't mind singing it.

We practiced with Miss Shahan. One benefit of this practice was Lulu's leaving me alone. I would have learned ten more Christian songs for that benefit alone. Praying, in any language or for any god, helps. I saw concrete results of prayer.

On Saturday night, after dinner, Miss Shahan led us three in single file to the stage and the four of us signed the "someone is crying Lord, kumbaya" and so forth. I kept looking at Miss Shahan to copy her in case I forgot the lines and also to avoid becoming nervous by looking at the audience.

Our song was a big hit. Everyone clapped and gave us a standing ovation. This was my first experience at getting praise in America. Americans are very generous in showering praise even at minor tasks. In India, getting praise is hard. You have to really earn it. In a similar situation, where a group of deaf people signed a song, the reception would be lukewarm at best. There would be snickers at "those unfortunate mutes," their flailing hands, and their attempt to get the Lord to help them.

We returned from Williamsburg after three days. I was tired, as were Lulu and Charmaine. The only person who was still fresh and full of energy was Miss Shahan. She had driven us for about three hundred miles and interpreted for us nonstop. We had done nothing except eat, sit around, watch her, and sing that famous song, which she directed and sang with us. She was, I guessed, about sixty years old. But she had more energy than the three young people dozing in the car while she drove with a smile fixed on her face.

17

Strange American Traditions

SOME AMERICANS THINK THEY DON'T HAVE TRADITIONS like Europe and other countries have and are proud of it. They claim proudly that they are too busy exploring new horizons to develop traditions, or so they say. However, I was stumped with some rituals that Americans practice.

The first is "homecoming." On Gallaudet campus, as in almost all American universities and colleges as well as in high schools, homecoming is a huge event. I spent a lot of time trying to understand what homecoming actually meant. Who was coming home? Where was the home? Why the big hoopla about it?

The *Buff and Blue*, the college newspaper, announced that Gallaudet would be playing football against Frostburg at my first homecoming. Who was Frostburg and why he, she, or it was coming home to Gallaudet was not clear to me despite my careful reading of the paper. Dan told me that "it was just another dumb thing" kids do. I was not satisfied and asked the same question of whomever had the patience to listen to stupid questions.

The first reaction was always the shock at the incredulousness of my question. These students had grown up hearing the word "homecoming" and understanding its meaning since they started going to school. This question must have been in the same category as "Where does the sun go every night?"

There were other things tied to this homecoming: the homecoming king and queen and princesses, a homecoming dance, a parade, and, of course, the football game. As this major event approached, academics took a backseat to this event.

I learned that Frostburg was a college and its football team was coming to play our team. A week before the game, the whole campus was plastered with banners bearing slogans like "Go Bisons," "Beat

Frostburg," and the like. What shocked me were the insults included in some of these banners. It was a friendly game between two colleges and the visiting team, as guests, should be treated with respect. The language and drawings on the banners were full of insults. For example, one huge banner showed Gallaudet's mascot, the bison, trampling the Frostburg mascot. My meek comments about this lack of civility were met with such ridicule that I shut up and just watched the whole show. I was fortunate for the "front row" seats for the whole event as I had to photograph every event.

There was a parade before the game. All classes and student organizations had built their own "floats." The beautiful girls chosen as homecoming queen and princesses sat in a convertible car and were driven around slowly as they waved to the crowd like real royalty. I wondered how much time and money the students had spent on building all of those for the parade. All of this ended with a homecoming dance. Not only were all the students there, but a large number of alumni had shown up. I walked around looking at people and saying hellos to those I knew. I got bored after an hour and went back to my room to sleep. So much for homecoming.

Then there were these Greek organizations. I was invited to a "rush" party by the Kappa Gamma Fraternity. I wondered who was in what rush but went to the party anyway. There were about twenty or thirty freshmen there. We were given lectures by the officers, which I didn't understand at all. The only part of the event I liked was the cookies and drinks served after the lecture. I asked a friend what it was about. He told me that this was a kind of orientation to Kappa Gamma, a fraternity on campus. I checked the dictionary about "fraternity" and learned it meant "brotherhood." What brotherhood? Why this strange name? There were many questions in my mind, but I was afraid to ask fearing ridicule.

One evening there was a big buzz about Kappa Gamma coming out. What was Kappa Gamma and where it was coming out from was a mystery, but I decided not to ask any stupid questions. I knew something very interesting was going to happen but was not prepared for what I saw.

Soon after the dinner, students crowded outside of Krug Hall. I ventured inside the lobby to see what it was about and got scared seeing about twenty persons dressed in colorful hooded robes with arms clasped in front descending the stairs slowly and purposefully. Where were they

At a Theta Nu Tau frat party.

going and what for? Their hoods made them very mysterious and scary. I could not believe they were Gallaudet students who went to classes with me. They looked like people from another planet. It took me a long time before I really understood the Greek organizations. I learned how these Greek organizations required scholarship, leadership, and other qualities for membership. I lost interest in the four Greek organizations as I learned that none of the members were from Greece and only a few were scholars or leaders. It was just a "fraternity." They picked who fit their mold. Existing members made sure their friends were initiated into the fraternity. Under the guise of leadership and scholarship, it was just another clique.

18

The First Christmas in America

AS CHRISTMAS APPROACHED, STUDENTS BEGAN TO TALK about going home. It seems that almost all students—except for few who could not afford to go home and, of course, foreign students—were leaving. Everyone asked me if I was going to India for the holiday and after a while I tired of telling them no. They had to understand that the roundtrip fare to India was three years of my father's income. The rupee went a long way in India, but in America, it shrank to oblivion.

Gallaudet remained open for the students who could not go home. We didn't have to pay additional charges. However, I needed money for purchasing books for the next semester. The money I had earned from my photography job went to expenses like washing clothes, cigarettes, and snacks. What was left was not enough. I needed $250 and my photography job would be in hiatus for a full month when the college was closed.

I went to see Thomas Berg, the assistant dean. His office was responsible for helping students find jobs. He told me to go to Woodward & Lothrop and Hecht's and gave me the addresses. I didn't know what these places were. Mr. Berg was in a hurry and also didn't understand why I wanted a job. He did make a comment: "We pay you full support, why do you want a job?" I told him about books and other expenses, but he still didn't appear convinced. I asked him if his secretary would call those places and get me an appointment. He told me the secretary was busy and I had to go there myself.

One didn't just show up at a place in India and ask for a job. I assumed it was different in America. The next day, after classes, I took a bus and found Woodward & Lothrop on 11th Street. It was a huge building, several stories high and spread over the whole block. I wondered what it was and entered the brass and glass revolving door with trepidation and found myself in a huge store. I had never seen such a huge store. The term "department store" had not yet been added to my vocabulary list.

What would I do in a department store? I walked around looking at all of those fancy clothes. Out of curiosity, I looked at some price tags and was shocked to see that some dresses cost more than what I might make working all year in the photography section at Gallaudet. "Who could afford those clothes?" I asked myself.

My stroll in the store finally brought me to an office. I asked a young lady about possible vacancies. She pointed to a corner desk and said something. I went there and found application forms for employment. That was very interesting. Instead of writing an application on a plain piece of paper, Americans had forms to fill out. I filled out the form and gave it to the lady. She waved me out with a smile.

The Hecht's store was just around the corner. It was the same story here. Fill out a form and leave it there. They would contact me if a job became available. I gave them the Ely Hall phone number to contact me.

Needless to say, neither Woodward & Lothrop nor Hecht's sent me an invitation to work. As Christmas neared, I got worried. I checked to see if my photography supervisor Frank could hire me during the break. He told me since the school would be closed, the question of my working there didn't arise.

I walked around the campus with a heavy heart as students began to leave at noon when the college closed for the holidays. Students were loading their bags in cabs for the airport. They were shaking hands and wishing "Merry Christmas" to each other. The atmosphere was full of joy. The end of the semester, the long vacation from classes, and the Christmas had made everyone happy. I was not. However, I shook hands, smiled, and wished them a nice vacation. I was happy for them or pretended to be.

The speed with which the campus became empty was amazing. By the time the sun set, which was early in December, the campus had less than ten people left and the only visible sign of life was the lone campus police cruiser crawling around eerily. I decided that worrying about people leaving and focusing on the creepy atmosphere in a once bustling campus would not help me buy books. I had to take some concrete action.

There were two Indian restaurants in Washington, DC. I had not visited either. It was time, I told myself, to check them out. I wore my better suit and put the overcoat that I had purchased at a Goodwill store over it. A check in the bathroom mirror assured me I looked professional and helped me feel confident.

I took a bus to Dupont Circle and then I walked on Connecticut Avenue until I saw the sign for the Taj Mahal on the second floor of a building. Slowly, I climbed the dark stairs and smelled Indian food being cooked. I was hungry and the smell made my stomach hurt. I had not eaten Indian food for more than four months and hoped that the restaurant manager would offer me a meal.

I emerged into a fancy dining room. The floor had plush red carpet and on the wall hung large Indian paintings. A waiter came forward with a menu, but I waved the menu aside and told him in English and with authority that I am here to see the manager. The waiter withdrew and went behind the kitchen door. A few minutes later an elegantly dressed young man came out with his hand extended. I shook it and very seriously told him, this time in Hindi, that I was deaf and was working on my MS at a local university and needed some work during the Christmas break to pay for my books. I had elevated my student status to get some respect. I kept talking without letting him say a word fearing that once he knew I could not lipread, I would be told to go away. I knew from experience that deaf people who could not talk or lipread were looked down upon in India.

The manager stood there wondering what to do. I told him he could write his response on a paper pointing to my right ear. He took a pen out of his jacket pocket and got a napkin and wrote, "We are very busy at the moment. Please come back tomorrow around 4 p.m. and I will see what job we can offer you." He ran away hastily after giving me the napkin.

The next day I arrived there half an hour earlier than the time he gave me. There was no staff person there and the elegant dining room was empty. I was looking at the paintings and other decorations and when I turned and saw a beautiful blonde woman standing a couple of feet from me looking puzzled and annoyed. Apparently, she had been trying to get my attention and was irritated that I was not responding.

I got all confused. What was an American woman doing in this Indian restaurant? I blurted that I was deaf and was here for the job that the manager had offered me yesterday. Her expression changed and she asked me to follow her to the other room. There we sat at a coffee table and she wrote questions and I responded. She was German, she said, and the wife of the owner. The owner had gone to England on business and had not told her anything about me. She was very nice and asked me to have dinner as their guest. But as to the job, she knew nothing.

I would have loved to have dinner there, but I was too upset about not getting the job to eat. I stood up and left without saying good-bye to her or even thanking her. She had been really nice and patient with me, but the feeling that my status here was no more than an unwanted beggar left me too depressed and angry for social niceties.

The atmosphere on Connecticut Avenue was festive. It was only 4:00 p.m., but the Christmas lights were already lit. The holiday spirit was in the air, but I didn't feel it. The thought that I wouldn't be able to buy books weighed heavily on me. I walked listlessly as I tried to think about what to do. I didn't want to go back to Gallaudet, as there was no one to talk to there and everything, including the library, was closed.

An idea struck me. Why not try other restaurants? There might be a job. I was too desperate to care what people thought about my barging in and asking for a job. I walked into the next place that looked like a restaurant. A waitress came forward with a menu in hand to welcome me. I was dressed in a suit and tie and looked like a dinner customer. I told her I was looking for a job as a waiter or a busboy. She didn't understand me, so I wrote on her little notebook. She shook her head indicating there was no job available. The same thing happened at the second and the third restaurant. I was thinking about going back to Gallaudet now but decided to try once more.

I liked the name of the next restaurant, the White Elephant. That was a bold statement. Was the food served in this restaurant very expensive and useless? Job or no job, I needed to go inside to see why they called it the White Elephant. It was a large bar actually. Two bartenders dressed in tuxedos were talking to three waitresses who were dressed like European maids. All of them were beautiful people, beautifully dressed. Despite my suit and tie, I felt shabby.

As I entered, one of the bartenders approached me with a menu in his hand and said something. I told him I was deaf and was looking for a job, expecting him to shake his head for not understanding me. But he understood me and said something in response. I told him that I was deaf and would he please write. He wrote on a napkin, the paper of choice in American restaurants, I thought.

"What can you do?" The usual question.

"I will work as a waiter or a busboy."

The five of them were looking at me and at each other. I thought it was time for one of them to point to the door through which I should leave, but instead they began to talk to each other animatedly. I stood there shifting from one foot to another waiting. Finally, the guy with the napkin and the pen wrote something and handed me the napkin.

"Can you wash dishes?" it read.

I did wash dishes in India a few times when I lived alone in Delhi, but my total production in the area of dish washing might have been about forty dishes in all. This bar might have more than that. And, of course, dishwashing is the lowest of low jobs in India. The same could be true in the United States. All of these thoughts came to my head while I was saying yes to him.

More discussions ensued and I was hired at $1.50 an hour starting right there and the offer was presented in one word on the napkin.

"I am Peter, the owner, this is my brother Jean." He pointed to the other tuxedo.

The three waitresses were also related to them. It was a family venture. They were from Hungary. Jean produced an apron from behind the counter and pointed toward a staircase leading up. I took the hint and found a small bathroom upstairs. As I took off my tie and jacket, I thought about Babuji, my father. Here I was a Brahman boy going to wash dishes. For centuries, no one in my family had even washed their own dishes, much less those of other people. I hoped Babuji would never know about it.

After putting on the apron, I went downstairs and was escorted to the kitchen where Jean introduced me to the cook. The cook showed a pile of dishes in a large sink, soap, pads, and towels. I stood there wondering what to do. Seeing my dilemma the cook came over to me and demonstrated how to wash a glass and then a pot. He worked fast with sure hands. I hoped to become as good as him at dishwashing.

The three weeks in White Elephant went well. I worked from 6:00 p.m. to 2:00 a.m. However, I only worked about four hours. The rest of the time, I sat and waited for dirty dishes to materialize. I brought books with me to read during the lull. At 1:30 or thereabout, I would be told to go.

The first night after work, I found the bus stand and waited for the bus. For almost thirty minutes there was no bus and I wondered if a bus really was coming. As I stood shivering, a car stopped and an elderly black man lowered the window, leaned from his driving seat over the passenger seat, and began to talk to me. I told him I needed to go to Gallaudet College. He pushed the door open and I got in.

I sat there quietly looking straight ahead and was thankful for the nice guy to give me the ride. Out of the corner of my eyes, I noticed the guy was talking to me. I told him I was deaf and continued looking straight ahead. Suddenly, he moved his hand and put it on my crotch, pressing the hand at the same time. I jumped from my seat and pushed his hand away. He brought his hand back and grabbed for my crotch. I yelled, "Stop the car. I want to get out," and forcibly pushed his hand away. He jerked the car to a stop and pushed me from the shoulder, telling me to get out. I was happy to get out. The car sped away before I could catch my balance.

I stood there in the empty street shivering from cold or from the strange experience I had. I was in Chinatown, I noticed. After getting my bearings and courage back, I started to walk to Gallaudet. It was only a little over two miles. I decided that hitchhiking is fine in the movies. In real life, either you don't get a lift or you wish you hadn't.

The job lasted me three or four weeks until the college reopened. Students were thrilled to be back. They were relating their holiday adventures. Some went skiing, some went to Florida. They also got lots of gifts for Christmas. I listened to those tales and wondered if I should tell them about my working in the White Elephant or the lift I got from that "nice" old guy.

There was a lot of talk about students who got academic dismissals. The group of students discussing these academic demises or survivals of friends and foes were boisterous. They clapped and jumped in joy when they learned that a student whom they didn't like wasn't coming back. These were the same students who had been so mature when I tried to play football and failed disastrously. I didn't understand why they took such pleasure at other students' failure.

Since the first semester was easy, I decided to take more classes to keep myself busy. My idea was to take twenty-one credit hours, but my advisor told me very nicely that I should not go over eighteen. The way this "advice" was presented was an excellent lesson in American kitchen diplomacy. Instead of telling me directly, "I don't think you're capable of carrying a load of twenty-one credits," I was told, "Well, perhaps you can do that, but I can't. I can't imagine myself carrying twenty-one credits of coursework in one semester." This coming from my advisor who already had a master's degree made this argument very powerful. I dropped the idea of carrying twenty-one credits. Looking back, I think I should have made a case for twenty-one credits and shaved one semester over three years. But my respect for professors was too strong to question their judgment.

19

Managing Finances

AS I SAID BEFORE, GALLAUDET HAD OFFERED ME A GRANT, which covered my tuition and room and board. I had to pay for my unit fees, which included charges for participation in various student organizations; the yearbook and some social activities; and books as well as for my upkeep. I had managed to meet these expenses by working part-time as a photographer and also by saving money during the summer working in the photography department full-time.

In addition to working at Gallaudet, I started working at the *Washington Post* on Wednesday and Saturday nights as an inserter. They hired about a hundred people to insert the advertisement section into the main newspaper. Most of the people working there were homeless and winos. A few of us Gallaudet students also joined this hapless group. It was not hard work. Of the eight hours we were required to work for about four hours as the machines frequently broke down and there were waiting periods as new news was added. During those off periods, we joked around.

I didn't spend money on anything except for food and managed to save about $600 out of the $700 I had earned. I didn't have a bank account, so I put the money in an envelope for my expenses next year.

The grant bothered me. I was never rich in India, but I had managed to carry my own weight. Now that I had $600 saved up, I decided to reduce my grant. When the school opened, I went to visit Mr. Phillips, the dean of students.

Mr. Phillips was in a hurry. "What do you want?"

"I want to discuss my grant," I said nervously while feeling the fat envelope in my pant pockets.

"I think we have awarded you full grant-in-aid. We can't give any more." He was gruff.

"No. No. I mean I want to pay some of my tuition myself." I stopped him from leaving his own office.

"What do you mean?" He was puzzled.

I brought out the envelope, placed it on his desk, and explained how I had saved up $600 from my summer work and wanted him to deduct it from my grant.

Mr. Phillips was puzzled. He looked at the envelope and then at me and again at the envelope. Then he picked it up and looked at the money inside and put it back on the desk and pushed it toward me as if it was dirty money.

"Take it back with you and put it in the Gallaudet Bank." He looked angry. "We can't take it. Use it for books, unit fees, and clothes." He was looking at me as if he was wondering about my sanity. I didn't understand it all, but I had in America only one year and still had high respect for authority. I obeyed, picked up the envelope, and went out of his office.

When I told the story of my humiliation in Mr. Phillips's office to some of my friends, they laughed and told me that I was the dumbest guy on earth. Some of them didn't even believe that I had offered my savings to Mr. Phillips. One friend even offered to help me by volunteering to take the envelope with the money from me and "put it to good use."

I put the money in the Gallaudet Bank right away and wondered what I would do with the money. However, after I had bought books and paid the unit fee, I had less than $300. I was glad that Mr. Phillips had not accepted the money or I would have been in a huge hole.

I learned an important lesson. In America, it seemed, you get what is given to you and ask for more. If you have money, you still can and should ask for more money. It was very hard for me to even think about asking for help when I had some money. However, I learned as I became more and more Americanized.

A dozen years later, when I decided to work on my doctoral degree, I began to save money to pay for my tuition and support the family. When I was confident that I had enough money, I started my studies. At that time, the chairman of the department told me that I would get a few thousand dollars as stipend for one year. I didn't tell him that I had already saved enough money to support my family. Instead, I thanked him for the support, which I "badly needed." I didn't feel bad or guilty. It was, as some of my friends say, "money for the taking."

20

The Foreign Students Group

GALLAUDET HAD OVER ONE THOUSAND STUDENTS DUR-
ing the 1960s, though only about twelve were from other countries,
not counting Canadians. Three were from the United Kingdom; three
from Africa; two from Japan; and one each from Germany, Hong Kong,
the Philippines, Belgium, and India. We shared a common sadness and
excitement about being away from home in a strange land and quickly
formed a close bond. We shared several challenges. We were away from
home and our families for a long time. We were adjusting to the American culture. Our friendship formed across boundaries of nationality, age,
gender, and race.

Enjoying Indian food with some other foreign students.

We formed an organization aptly named the Foreign Students Club. We staged cultural shows with folk dances and food, showed international movies, and even had our float in the homecoming parade. It was a simple float. Some of us sat in an open car, dressed in our native clothes and bearing some flags borrowed from our embassies. We were small in number but very active and visible as individuals and as a group. The dean's list included 90 percent of foreign students almost each semester. We were all very serious about our studies, as we didn't study for ourselves but for our countries. The grade point average of a Japanese student reflected the cumulative academic achievement of the country. Hartmut, the lone German student, had to excel in science and mathematics. Chuzo and Michiko, two Japanese students, majored in mathematics. At the end of my freshman year, a teacher thought I was majoring in chemistry, the subject I hated most. He told me that I had made so much progress during the year that he thought I should continue. I thought about it for about ten minutes and decided that chemistry was not my cup of tea.

The foreign boys didn't play football and the girls didn't become cheerleaders. They didn't participate in "pure American" activities such as Sadie Hawkins Day or betting on the World Series finalists. They did join various campus groups and organizations, including the Greeks. None of the foreign students were ever really accepted as mainstream Gallaudet students. We were smart, we were cute, and we were friendly, but we were never full-fledged and bona fide Gallaudetians. Our roots were too deep in our respective cultures and it would take years to change us for full assimilation. The fact that Hartmut acted in a play and won the best actor award was an anomaly.

As I look back, being up close with these foreign students was an education unto itself. We learned about each other's countries, educational systems, and the lives of deaf people around the world. One can't learn all that by reading books or watching documentaries. The personal explanations based on growing up in a country are unparalleled. I look back with great delight to those bull sessions discussing our countries. Of course, we were not short of insulting each others' countries based on stereotypes we had developed. I got my share of barbs about India's poverty, caste system, snake charmers, and elephants.

Most of these "foreign" students were not foreign for long. Except for two or three, all of us stayed in America. They all have jobs, married, and have children, just like any other American. The Gallaudet foreign students were just like other immigrants who came to America, except that we were here for an education and with serious plans to return home to do great things. As time passed, the visions, the dreams, and the grand plans faded as the American dream took over. How did it happen? No one knows; it just grew on us without our knowledge. Even if you do not have an American Dream, the American Dream will have you.

While a lot of things about America piqued our curiosity, American football was a mystery that most of us could not understand. All of us grew up on the football that the Americans called "soccer." We used to go to the Gallaudet home football games just because everyone else went and were excited despite the fact that Gallaudet lost almost all the games. We would look at the scoreboard showing Gallaudet being humiliated by a team that had not won a single game that season and then look at the cheerleaders who would be jumping with joy.

In real football, known as soccer here, players played nonstop. There is an occasional shout from one player to another or instruction from the sideline by coaches. The rest is all work. In American football, the team playing offense huddles after each play and goes into deep discussions with their heads bent down and arms around each other. For us that was a mystery and we always wondered what exactly they discussed. One day we had our opportunity in the huddle, finally. The huddles we had experienced in our PE classes did not count; we never knew what was going on.

During my first summer, all the foreign students working on campus were housed in the empty houses next to House One, where Dr. Elstad, the president of Gallaudet, lived. All the boys lived in House Three and the girls in House Four. There were two or three American boys in our house and several American girls lived in the girls' house. In the evening we all would get together on one of the houses' porches and talk about nothing special.

A few houses from the house we lived in was Frank Turk's house. He was the dean of Gallaudet's preparatory department. One evening we were talking and watching Frank's son throwing a football around when one of the American girls suggested that we play football. The idea was to have a game between the American girls and the foreign boys. Our experience in playing football was limited to learning it in PE class for a couple of weeks. We had managed to forget the intricacies of the game a long time before. However, we accepted the challenge.

The game began with the girls taking the offense. They discussed their strategy in the huddle and then they lined up. These American girls knew what they were doing. They had a plan and easily scored a touchdown with a pass play on their first down. We were embarrassed and blamed each other for paying more attention to looking at the girls than the ball. However, that touchdown proved to be beginner's luck. We managed to check their progress after that and got the ball.

Getting the ball was one thing and doing something with it was another. Sambo, who was from Nigeria, clamed to know something about football. What exactly he knew was a mystery to us, including probably to Sambo. Chuzo, from Japan, had spent a year in the Wisconsin School for the Deaf and had become good friends with several football players there. He suggested that we form a huddle first. We formed it and took a lot of time doing that as we wanted to make sure our huddle was perfect. We were pushing and instructing each other on the art of huddle formation. The American girls were laughing hysterically and one was even rolling on the grass.

Sambo took the leadership role by default. He was the best soccer player among us. He took a look at the laughing girls and then told Chuzo, the quarterback, to throw the ball to him.

"Where will you be?" Chuzo asked.

"I'll be here and won't run to Nigeria. Just look at me and throw the ball." Sambo admonished him.

"But," Chuzo, who knew football, said, "you have to pick a side to run so I can throw the ball there."

"OK," relented Sambo, "you see that girl with big boobs jumping in her red t-shirt? Just throw the ball to her."

Chuzo was upset. He tried to explain that the ball is supposed to be thrown to one of the team members. But Sambo didn't care. He told Chuzo to the throw the ball to the girl as he wanted to tackle her to the ground. The fact that Sambo was more interested in tackling the girl and her sizeable assets than in the ball upset Chuzo. However, we were all laughing at Sambo's strategy and asked Chuzo to follow his directions. He gave in to the majority as he was a firm believer in democracy.

Sambo's game strategy worked. The American girls seemed to be more interested in tackling and being tackled. The ball bounced from here to there and no throws were caught. However, we all had fun. After half an hour, we were all tired and drenched in sweat. We agreed to play the game every evening. However, that was the first and last American football match we played. We all got busy with other activities and forgot about American football.

These friendships among the foreign students, however, lasted only the first one or two years. We all became Americanized and found American friends. The problems we faced in the beginning slowly became less important and participating in the various activities that Gallaudet offered became more important and also brought us closer to our American friends.

Gallaudet has hundreds of foreign students now. Instead of creating one club for all foreign students, now there are clubs for each region or even each country. There are a large number of students who were born in the United States to parents who had, like us foreign students of 1960s, immigrated to America. Despite their being born here, they are still foreign. They still join various clubs that represent the country from which their parents came.

21

Fort Gallaudet

BY THE SECOND SEMESTER AT GALLAUDET, I HAD GOTTEN into the flow of college life. The twenty-six years I had spent in India were a hazy memory. The busy life at Gallaudet had me absorbed fully. Classes, homework, a part-time job, extracurricular activities, and friends occupied my time and India became a distant country. I did not think about India much nor did I miss my life there anymore. I thought about my wife often though and wondered if there was a way to bring her to America. The only way she could move here would have been for me to get a well-paying job that would support living off campus. Since most of the grant would stop if I moved off campus, I had to push this idea into the background. Our only contact was by mail. It took about two or three weeks for a letter to reach India. So we had, perhaps, ten letter exchanges a year.

As the semester progressed and summer vacation was approaching, suddenly the bucolic atmosphere of Gallaudet was shattered by the assassination of Reverend Martin Luther King, Jr.

I had read a little about Dr. King mostly because of his references to Mahatma Gandhi. As an Indian, it was a matter of pride for me that an American leader was emulating the Gandhian principle of nonviolent confrontation. I was hoping that Dr. King would use *satyagraha* (nonviolent resistance) to get equal rights for black people. The parallel between Gandhi's freedom of struggle and Dr. King's efforts, however, was little. Gandhi wanted to get rid of the colonial empire by asking the British to leave India; Dr. King wanted equality.

Dr. King was assassinated in the evening on April 4, 1968. I didn't watch television and only read the *Washington Post* sporadically. There was only one television in our dormitory and it was mostly turned off. The only time it had a number of watchers was when a game was on.

No wonder I didn't learn about Dr. King's assassination until the next morning.

All classes were dismissed and students milled around the campus in groups talking about the assassination. Gallaudet at that time had only about four or five black students. Only two of them were visible as one of them was a star gymnast and the other a star basketball player. That was Glenn Anderson, who later became the chairman of the board of trustees.

No one really discussed Dr. King on campus; however, his assassination now made him the main topic of discussions. I tried to understand what was being said in various groups and was surprised that most students didn't know much about Dr. King, either. There were some racist remarks about him for being "uppity" and a troublemaker. Very few students talked about him as a leader with a vision.

The excitement and joy caused by this unexpected cancellation of classes didn't last long. We had nothing to do because we couldn't leave campus and the campus didn't offer much excitement. The Rathskeller, the now-popular drinking place, was not even an idea at that time. Bowling and pinball machines were the only attractions.

It was not long, however, before excitement came to Gallaudet. The H Street area where we shopped for snacks and sundry goods such as soap and toothpaste went up in flames. We saw a wall of black smoke curling toward the sky from that direction. We all got scared and wondered if these fires would spread to Gallaudet's campus. There was no order on campus. There were no assemblies or meetings to explain what was going on to us students. Our only communication source from the outside world was the *Washington Post* and the *Washington Star*. The *Star* was published in the evening. The television showed coverage of violence in various cities and it did little to assuage our fears. The dormitory supervisors' offices were crowded with students who wanted the supervisors, the only hearing people on campus now, to make calls to their parents about their safety. The only phone in each office was busy responding to incoming calls from worried parents. I wondered about my own family. Babuji, being an avid reader of several newspapers, would have learned about the assassination and the resulting violence. Newspaper stories must have made it sound much worse than it was. I had no way of contacting him. Gagret still didn't have a telephone and I couldn't send a telegram from Gallaudet. Going into downtown to a telegraph office was out of the question.

The joy and excitement of cancelled classes gave way to panic on campus. The students weren't laughing or chatting any more. They were worried and talked about how long this would last. Some of those who didn't like Gallaudet much thought the placement of Gallaudet in the middle of a ghetto was stupid. All kind of talk was going on and I just watched them and wondered how students would have reacted in an Indian college over the assassination of a national leader.

This mood was then broken by four army helicopters landing on the football field. The bored students flocked to the bleachers. None of us had ever imagined seeing army helicopters on campus. I had never even seen a helicopter that close.

The helicopters landed and about fifty uniformed soldiers jumped out of them one by one. We had no classes and television programs were not captioned. This arrival of the army right on our football field was fascinating. It was also the only game in town.

The soldiers pitched tents on the football field. Some of them stood guard and the rest moved around setting up the camp. We all watched the process with great interest. Soon the soldiers began to point at the staring students. They must have seen us signing and were wondering about it. The students and the soldiers kept their distance during the first day. On the second day, when the soldiers felt more settled, some of the hard of hearing students begin to talk to them and explain about deafness and signing.

The soldiers never left the perimeter of the football field and students never ventured into it. We felt safer due to the presence of the soldiers. They were there just to protect us. However, a lot of communication, mostly visual, was going on between the soldiers and the students. The main communication was between the girls and the soldiers who stared and smiled at the pretty girls who would stare back, giggle, and hide behind their female friends. The boys joined the game and would drag a girl, who flailed her arms and legs helplessly, to the front and point her to the laughing soldiers to take her. This went on for hours.

The fires on H Street were gone after two days. The soldiers stayed for five or six days and then folded their tents and flew back in the helicopters. The classes started after five days and life became normal again. Fort Gallaudet, as students had begun to call the college, was no more.

One result of this short stay of soldiers was that one Gallaudet student became a steady friend of one soldier and a year later, she married him. I met that student thirty or more years later and learned that she was still married to him. The student was not hard of hearing. She couldn't lipread and the soldier didn't know signs. How they communicated is a mystery. But communicate they did and continued the communication all the way to the altar.

22

Education Outside the Classroom

AS I WROTE EARLIER, MOST OF WHAT I LEARNED AT GAL-
laudet was outside the classroom. Since my deafness, I was forced to be my
own teacher. I learned what interested me and learned when I was interested. Being part of a teacher's captive audience for fifty minutes I found
was not very conducive to learning. However, I never cut one class. I sat in
the front row dutifully "listening" to each lecture with an eager expression
as my mind drifted a million miles away. During each fascinating class session, I outdreamed Walter Mitty. I did manage to ask one or two questions
in each class so the teacher would feel I was genuinely interested.

I was learning a lot, however! People learn by doing things and talking about them. Gallaudet offered a lot of opportunities to participate in
a number of extracurricular activities. During my first year, I started as
the photographer for the *Buff and Blue*, the college newspaper. This was
in addition to my photography job. I didn't participate in other activities
as I was not sure how much time schoolwork would take. After feeling
the ropes during the first semester, I felt comfortable in joining various
activities in addition to working twenty hours a week in the audiovisual
department.

I signed up to play soccer mainly due to pressure from my friend Leslie from Scotland. He was the captain of the team and a great player. The
team was made up of foreign players, including Canadians.

I had not played soccer since I left Gagret and even then it was sporadic.
There was no soccer field or team in Gagret and we didn't even have a
soccer ball, so we played with rag balls or tennis balls. Even though I was
already twenty-seven and not very athletic, the pressure to join the Gallaudet team was huge, so I joined. Needless to say, I warmed the bench
during the whole year. My career as a soccer player was short-lived and
painful—both physically and mentally.

But I learned a lot while practicing and playing. We players developed close bonds and had fun while not playing. I also learned that in America a coach does not need to know how to play the game. Our first coach, Mr. Bushnaq, fell down every time he tried to show us how to play. The fact that he had a cigarette in his mouth all the time didn't help. Another coach, Mr. Minter, had never played soccer but knew all the rules from his classes. He had majored in PE, after all.

In addition to becoming president of the Foreign Students Club, I also served as the managing editor of the *Buff and Blue*, class representative for the student body government and member of several committees. These activities didn't cost me much time but provided me opportunities to learn communication and discussion skills. I lacked those because herding cattle in Gagret and plowing the fields behind a team of oxen were not fertile grounds to develop such skills. I felt really slow and stupid while sitting in those meetings watching other members overflowing with ideas—both smart and dumb—and sharing those eloquently. In India, we discussed issues informally and our conversations were short and to the point. All of those ideas that sounded so new to me were actually old ones. I was just in a new country. I could not get the nerve to get up and talk in front of other students for almost a year. Later, I began to feel more comfortable and started expressing my ideas.

As I look back, these extracurricular activities helped in my career as a teacher and administrator. Standing in front of a class or the whole school requires self-confidence and the ability to think on one's feet. Serving on these committees helped me develop these skills.

The other productive learning opportunities were in the Student Union Lounge and dormitory lounges. The students talked and discussed things that were important and totally insignificant. They discussed politics, sports, girls, and issues specific to Gallaudet such as teachers, not necessarily in that order. Usually I listened as I really didn't understand it all. American politics were new to me and the issue of the Vietnam War was never clear. Vietnam, which overshadowed all other issues in the newspapers and on television, was never a major issue at Gallaudet since deaf persons were exempt from the military draft.

The breadth and depth of discussions was amazing. There were some students who spent most of their time talking about their favorite issues late into the night. These were also the students who slept most of the morning, cut classes regularly, and, when they did attend, slept in the back of the class. These were smart students and learned a lot on their own. The obligatory attendance to classes was not their top priority. Some of them openly disparaged the teachers.

I didn't participate in these hot discussions and usually left in the middle of such talks, since I didn't enjoy marathon discussions. I did manage to learn something from these, perhaps more than I learned attending all of those classes dutifully. The difference was that I slept with my eyes open in classrooms and paid attention to these informal discussions.

23

Seeing America

SINCE I WAS TO BE IN AMERICA FOR ONLY SIX YEARS, I wanted to see as much of America as I could. My means were limited, but travel was in my blood, so each summer I managed to see one part or another of America. My friends helped in this effort by providing free car rides or hospitality in their homes if I passed through their city.

The first trip was to Assateague Island near Ocean City, Maryland. It was a beautiful island, all sand dunes and tall grass. This was my first experience seeing a wild beach. Kirk, whom I had met when I first went to Ely Hall after learning that I was a freshman, was from California. He was one of the few people who used to stop me to have a chat while passing each other. He was also one of the few students who knew something about India and didn't ask me if I shared my residence with cows or if I hung from the trees with monkeys. It took me a while to learn that Kirk was hearing. In India, very few hearing people signed and none fluently. Therefore I always thought whoever signed fluently was deaf. I used Sim-Com as a habit and when Kirk began to correct my pronunciations, I was surprised.

"Are you hard of hearing?" I asked as Dan also corrected my English pronunciations.

"No. I am hearing." He later told me that he had met a deaf guy when he was a teenager, struck up a friendship with him, and learned to sign. He ended up working on his MA in deaf education.

One day, Kirk stopped me and asked if I would like to go camping. Camping was totally foreign to me. I had a faint idea about tents and cooking on campfires. Camping was for soldiers in wars. I never thought one went on camping just for the sake of camping. I thought, "why not?" and said, "yes."

Kirk had a jeep and he borrowed a pop-up camper from a friend. He had also invited his friends Willis and Jackie Mann. Jackie was Kirk's classmate and Willis had graduated from Gallaudet a year earlier and was working on a graduate degree in the University of Maryland. Kirk and I met Willis and Jackie at their apartment and together we set off for camping. Kirk explained that we would use this pop-up camper to sleep in and that we would cook on a gas stove or wood fire. I was wondering all the way to the island why Americans leave behind their air-conditioned homes and all their worldly comforts to go camping. When I shared my musings with Kirk, he laughed. He had no answer, and, I guess, he did not know why they did that. They suffer heat and humidity, mosquito bites, flies, and ticks at the campground. Instead of cooking food on the range, they cook slowly on a gas stove. After working hard, earning money, and purchasing all their luxury goods, Americans go camping to get a taste of how people in Gagret live and they pay for it. I wondered.

It was actually nice to be out camping on the beach. Being outside in the open air was refreshing. I never got tired looking at the blue ocean and walking on the beach. However, it was too cold to swim. Eating bacon and eggs straight from the skillet was a new experience. The food tasted a lot better than what we ate in the Gallaudet cafeteria. There is something to be said about freshly cooked food. We walked on the beach and looked for wild ponies, which we could not find. After two days of camping, we returned to the lap of luxury. Needless to say, I decided that camping was fine for an experience and I had that under my belt. No more camping for me. I had camped enough with the cattle in India and spending my time looking for ticks kind of ticked me off.

In the summer of 1968, Sambo and I decided to "explore America." With our limited means and little knowledge of America, we decided to visit New York City. We had grown up seeing the skyscrapers in photographs. The idea of seeing the world-famous city and walking its streets exhilarated us. We knew nothing about where to stay and what exactly to see, so we asked Gabriel, my roommate who was also from Nigeria, to help us, as he had visited New York City a year earlier.

I typed a formal letter with the usual "dear sir" and "yours faithfully" to the YMCA near Columbia University and reserved two rooms for us for $4.50 per day. Sambo and I bought tickets on Trailways for $16 each way and boarded the huge bus to New York City dressed in our best suits, ties, and shoes. We looked at the never-ending stream of cities and towns and waited patiently to see the world-famous skyline of Manhattan.

We did finally see it as our bus emerged from the Lincoln Tunnel. We saw it only for two seconds before other buildings obscured the amazing site. It was not the Taj Mahal, but it is close to it.

We had to use a common bathroom, but that was just like living in a dormitory and we didn't mind. The room charges included a "continental breakfast." We didn't know what it included, but the word "continental" impressed us and we were sure it was substantial. The next morning, we dressed up in our best suits and dress shoes and looked for the breakfast place. In the cafeteria we both loaded up our trays and presented the ticket for the free "continental breakfast." The cashier rang up a few dollars for both of us. We were stumped. The cashier pointed at the doughnut, juice, and the coffee. That was a "continental" breakfast. We put all other stuff except for the donut, coffee, and orange juice back, as the cost of other items we had picked up was close to our daily room charge.

The next three days went by in a haze. We used the subway to get around town and ate in the Automat cafeterias. Everything in these cafeterias was stocked in vending machines lined against the three walls. They were cheaper and we did not have the hassle of dealing with people who expected us to lipread them.

We went up the Empire State Building, which was the tallest building in the world at that time. The view from the top was amazing. I hoped it would rain, so we could see the rain fall from the sky. But it was a clear day. Coney Island, however, was a disappointment. For some unknown reason, it was deserted. No one was there, the stores were closed, and rides stood idle. We photographed each other in front of the United Nations building and other famous places. When we got tired, we rode the subway until we had rested enough to visit another site.

The one word that I could think of to describe New York City was "big." Everything was big. The city seemed to stretch in every direction. The tall buildings, the endless rides in the subway, the huge ferries that carried cars and people, and the number of people all combined to make me think of NYC as big.

It was August and New York was hot and humid, but we never took off our jackets and ties. Walking in dress shoes was a chore, but we could not think of dressing down while visiting New York City. We had to dress nice to visit the world famous city. By the end of the third day we were exhausted. We took the Trailways bus and returned to Gallaudet. We both felt and acted like world travelers and walked with a swagger that can only come after one has climbed the world's tallest building, stood in front of the U.N. headquarters, and walked on the beach of Coney Island. We told tales of our visit to other students with great flourish. They were more amused than impressed but listened to us politely.

24

Travels in America

ONE OF MY GOALS WAS TO SEE ALL FIFTY STATES DURING my time at Gallaudet. Despite the little money I had, I hoped I could at least visit the forty-eight contiguous states. The only way I could achieve this goal was to travel with friends who had cars or use the wonderful American invention called hitchhiking. My two efforts at hitchhiking were total failures. I waited for hours and no one stopped. I noticed other people being picked up and also noticed the gimmicks they used. An attractive girl would strike a pose with her thumb out while the guys with her were standing away from her. I gave up and looked for opportunities of traveling with friends. My big opportunity after the short trip to NYC with Sambo came in the summer of 1969.

Kirk, the graduate student from California and of the camping experience, caught me in the hallway one day and asked if I was interested in going to California with him. Kirk was graduating in May and was going back home for a job. The word California got me all excited, followed by the big damper when I thought about money or rather the lack of it. Kirk must have read my expression and he smiled.

"You do not have to pay for anything except for your food," he said.

"What about the hotel on the way?" I asked.

"No hotels, Sahib." Kirk liked to throw in colonial vocabulary. "We will be camping."

"You mean," I asked, "you will pull that funny camper behind your jeep all the way to California?"

"No," laughed Kirk, "that wasn't mine to begin with. We will be using my pup tent for sleeping."

I wondered what a pup tent was. The other tent that had emerged from a huge box on wheels and produced two queen-sized beds was called a pop-up camper. After doing some linguistic gymnastics in my head, I concluded this pup tent would have only one queen-sized bed.

Without thinking further, I moved my closed fist in an up-and-down motion to convey a resounding "yes."

This was a free trip, since I had to eat wherever I was, so the food wasn't exactly an expense. I didn't think of other indirect expenses. Going on a "free" trip is like buying a car. There are always other expenses. I didn't think of the wages I was going to lose while traveling and didn't think about how I would get back to Gallaudet. Kirk wasn't coming back. At that time, however, I was too excited to think about anything else except seeing California.

"Will we go through Texas?" was an important question I asked.

"Yes," Kirk said, "you can see Zane Grey's world."

There was no turning back now. I was going. The idea of seeing cattle stampeding, the Rio Grande, saloons, and cowboys with ten-gallon hats sent me dreaming.

"Can you drive?" Kirk brought me back to earth.

"Yes." I lied. I could drive a little, but moving a car from here to there and driving on an American highway in a Jeep are not the same. But the idea of driving got me more excited than traveling itself. I didn't want to look backward, so decided to fib about my driving ability.

"But," the truth took over, "I don't have an American driving license." I forgot to mention that I didn't have an Indian driving license, either. All for a good cause.

"Good." Kirk was happy. "You can spell me when I am tired." Little did Kirk know the kind of spell he was going to experience.

To travel in America in style and to blend with the locals when we passed through Texas, I decided to buy two pairs of jeans and two denim shirts to go with them. I wanted to look rugged. That was a mistake. One looks rugged only after the clothes have seen some rugged time. In the beginning, I looked like a cowboy going for his first dance or getting married; this was not the look I wanted.

I packed a small bag with three changes of clothes, my camera, and a kit for brushing my teeth and shaving. Kirk packed his jeep with his clothes, books, and sports goods. Kirk, who claimed to be a *sadhu* (an Indian holy man), had much more baggage than twenty *sadhus* put together. However, he had much less stuff than a typical graduate student returning home. It is all relative.

"I'll drive first," said Kirk as he got into the driver's seat. "You'll take over when I'm tired." I nodded affirmatively with a broad smile to hide my fear.

So we took off. This was my second experience traveling on American highways. The trip to Williamsburg and Jamestown was on mostly flat roads bordered by small towns and farmland. This trip took me through mountains and deserts. I saw from the open window of Kirk's jeep the wonder that is America. I had brought a few books with me to read while traveling, but I could never read them. The only book I read was Kirk's copy of the road atlas. America is huge, but one does not actually realize its hugeness until one takes a road trip in an open jeep as it swallows the yellow ribbon of the road, spends nights at the roadside rest areas or small campgrounds, and sees how the landscape changes.

When we hit the Pennsylvania Turnpike, I was amazed at the curving highway snaking through the mountains. Kirk drove at seventy miles per hour and looked as relaxed as someone meditating. I held the door handle for dear life and pressed hard with my both feet on nonexistent brakes while trying to look relaxed. Kirk was smiling seeing my body language. He grew up driving fast cars during the era in which the famous movie *American Graffiti* was based.

"Are you not afraid driving on these S-curves that fast?" I finally asked, admitting that I was afraid was a hard job.

Kirk smiled. "We Americans are made of different stuff. Nothing about peace and meditation."

No more talks of driving after that. I developed a strong fear, however. The idea of my driving on these roads sent a cold wave up my spine. I thought about the jeep landing in a ravine and going up in flames.

We stopped for lunch at a truck stop. Kirk explained that truck stops served good food at reasonable prices. I agreed even though I didn't think that the food was good or the price reasonable. I longed for dal and chapati that one could buy in a roadside *dhaba* (a cheap greasy spoon) in India for twenty-five cents. These meals in truck stops cost about two or three dollars. I had to remind myself that I was in America and the minimum wage here was higher than what a college professor in India earned at that time.

After lunch, Kirk tossed the jeep keys to me and asked me to drive for an hour so he could rest. I climbed on to the driver's seat, which was set for Kirk's six-feet-plus tall frame. Kirk had to help me adjust the seat and then wait patiently while I fiddled with the keys. I started and shifted gears as the jeep jumped like a bronco. Kirk laughed, more to hide his fear than to encourage me, I thought.

I brought the jeep onto the road and while trying to shift from first to second gear also shifted the steering wheel. The jeep lurched to the left instead of forward. Kirk pulled at the steering wheel in time to keep the jeep on the right side. Fortunately, there was no traffic from the opposite direction.

"This is not India." Kirk tried to laugh. "In America, for your information, we drive on the right side."

Looking at him signing didn't help. I began to steer erratically. I learned while looking at Kirk sideways that Americans are fearless only when they are driving. Giving your car keys, and safety, to a former Indian farmer made bravery, or acting brave, obsolete.

After a few minutes of my driving and not seeing any improvement, Kirk signaled me to pull over, which I did in a hurry. I was breathing heavily and also sweating. I had only driven for four or five minutes, but it seemed like ages. We got out and exchanged seats quietly. I sat staring at the yellow divider and didn't say anything for a long time. I was embarrassed about my driving skills and also about lying that I could drive. Kirk sensed my discomfort and remained quiet. However, he never let me forget about the "great joy ride" he had with the "ace Indian driver." The story was told and retold during our trip.

25

A Week with Hippies

KIRK WAS IN A HURRY TO REACH NEW MEXICO. I ASKED him what was in New Mexico. He said, "Friends." Kirk changed from being the most cheerful and garrulous person in the world to the most grumpy and taciturn. I learned to read his moods and play along. When he took time answering my questions or gave monosyllabic answers, I would stop asking questions and become very interested in the road atlas or the yellow ribbon on the road as the jeep swallowed it.

I wanted to see Texas, but it was a blur. We passed through the panhandle area and all I could see were signs for "all-you-can-eat steak" restaurants or some tourist traps. Kirk vehemently refused to stop and see those places. "Those are for suckers," he told me. I did not mind being a sucker for once, but it was his jeep and he made the decisions. I missed the cattle drives of Red River and huge oil rigs of *Giant*. Of course, there were no gun-toting cowboys or the saloons with swinging doors. I decided to return later to see the real Texas.

We arrived in Albuquerque, which I pronounced "al-boo-kwe-rkew," and was corrected by Kirk as "al-baw-kerk," I saw a very different city than any I had seen in America. The adobe houses with their thick mud-colored walls and flat roofs reminded me of homes in Punjab. The doors were also designed similarly. I wondered why there was so much similarity. Then I saw a tortilla in a restaurant and thought of chapatis. The food was spicy and served hot like in India, but a different kind of hot. Instead of chutney, they had salsa. But the base was still the fiery red pepper. I felt at home.

Kirk needed to get his jeep fixed as the shocks were worn out. We spent most of the day lounging around Albuquerque and visiting with John Roberts, a Gallaudet student from the city. Late in the afternoon, the jeep was ready and we left for San Ysidro, where his friend lived. A strange name for a city, I thought. It was my first exposure to the Spanish language, I thought. I was reeling from Albuquerque and now this. It seemed like Americans didn't like simple names for cities like Delhi, Bombay, or Ram Pur.

The road toward San Ysidro was very beautiful with dry mountains on both sides. There were small dry-looking trees. It was almost a desert. I had never thought of mountains being dry. A mountain or a hill always meant tall green trees. This was a new world.

Kirk consulted the road map and took the jeep off-road at one point. There wasn't a road; there were just barely visible tire tracks that Kirk followed. The jeep bounced up and down and swayed from side to side as he drove at five miles per hour. I held on to the strap overhead and wished we were doing seventy miles per hour like we had on the turnpike. We went through a ravine filled with sand and rocks, which was not very different from Gagret. There was no human beings or houses visible. The evening was drawing fast and the long shadows of dry bushes made the landscape look scary.

After about twenty minutes, we saw a shack. Kirk beamed and told

Teaching signs to the hippies.

me that he thought his friend was there. I couldn't believe someone was living in that shack. It was America, famous for skyscrapers.

Kirk halted the jeep next to the shack and jumped out. I stood there wondering what would emerge from the shack. A young man with long, curly hair, wearing a pair of jeans and no shirt came out and jumped at Kirk. They both hugged and went around and around. This was the first time I saw Kirk hug another man. Actually, this was the first time I saw two American men hug each other and not be called "queer."

I walked slowly toward the hugging men and saw seven or eight more people materialize from the shack. All of them were topless, including two women. They all were smiling as Richard, the hugger, introduced Kirk and then Kirk began to sign and introduced me to them. Kirk emphasized that I was from India. They seemed to be so happy. One of them said something and Kirk laughed.

"He said, 'om,'" Kirk interpreted.

I was surprised that in this wild place, these young men and women were chanting "om." And then another young woman appeared with a baby in her arms. The young woman was hardly sixteen or seventeen years old and was very beautiful. Like the other women, she was topless. She joined her hands in the traditional Indian greeting, "namaste." I didn't feel at home with this greeting as I was disconcerted with this nonchalant show of upper torso.

The shack had two large rooms with a dirt floor. There was no electricity, no running water, and no furniture. They drew water from a shallow well and submerged a gallon jug of milk with a rope in the cool water. That was their "refrigerator." The only mode of transportation was walking. They were living like the *sadhus* in India.

Richard said something to Kirk and Kirk asked me to follow them. We ran after Richard, who was full of vim and vigor. He laughed; he jumped around and talked animatedly. We ran a few hundred yards to a shallow muddy river, the Rio Puerco. The setting sun was as red as I had ever seen it. It was simply beautiful. I took pictures while Richard danced around splashing the muddy water on Kirk and Kirk splashed back. They were like two kids.

We stayed for four or five days in San Ysidro as Kirk became very sick after a day there. The well water didn't agree with him. I walked around and talked to the residents there. All of them had long hair, long beards, and nothing with them except for the clothes on their backs, or rather, on their legs, as they didn't wear shirts. Their prized possessions were three or four pipes, which were lit most of the time and passed around.

There was Dave, a thin, tall blond boy of about eighteen. He was from California. There was Wayne, a younger boy with a shock of curly brown hair that stood a foot above his head. I do not remember the others, as they talked little. Dave and Wayne learned to finger spell and could communicate with me slowly. I taught signs and finger spelling to all, but only Dave and Wayne practiced.

After Kirk got better, we decided to move on. He had planned to stay here only for one day but had to stay for four days. He said he had another friend, Judy, in Santa Fe and wanted to see her. So we drove the jeep over sand and rocks again to hit a highway back to America. The little shack with its people had made me forget about the Empire State Building, millions of cars rushing on the endless ribbons of highways, and the hustle bustle of busy people running to nowhere. It was a different world.

Dave and Wayne decided to join us. They both wanted to go back home to California. Wayne explained to me in his slow finger-spelled words that he was homesick and missed his family. I asked him if his parents knew where he was, he shook his head sadly.

"If they knew where I was, they would come and get me or tell the police," he said.

"Why did you run away?" I was puzzled why a nice kid like him who was happy with his family had to run away.

"I wanted to find myself," he said.

This "finding myself" was the reason given by a lot of young people I met. That was the famed 1960s when most young people in America were trying to "find" themselves. Wayne was angry with his parents and was also worried about being drafted. So he had decided one day to join a group of young people who were planning to go to New Mexico to "find themselves."

After two months of wandering, he still had not found himself. However, he found things he wasn't looking for: hunger, pot, the shallowness of people, and, most of all, appreciation for all his parents had done for him. He was going back home and was sorry for putting his parents through all of this. In a way, I thought, he had found himself.

Now the jeep with Kirk and I sitting up front and Wayne and Dave lying on Kirk's belongings was really full. However, soon we had more travelers joining us. Kirk kept adding hitchhikers until Wayne, Dave, and I were sharing the front seat and four people lay on Kirk's clothes and books. Indian buses were less crowded.

Santa Fe was a different place than San Ysidro. I was captivated with the beautiful buildings and Native Americans selling jewelry on the sidewalk. What impressed me the most was the blueness of the sky. The clean, crisp air made the sky look very close and very blue. I ended up taking pictures of the sky itself.

We stayed with Judy for one night. She had known Kirk for many years in California and had graduated from Gallaudet a few years earlier. I played with Jerry, her eight-year-old daughter. This was the first time I had played with an American kid. There were no kids at Gallaudet.

We hit the road again, this time to California. Kirk decided to drive straight with stops for gas and bathroom breaks only.

We made it to Los Angles in two days with a stop at a roadside rest area where Kirk took a short nap. I wanted to see Hollywood and Disneyland, but Kirk was in a hurry. After dropping off everyone except Wayne and me in Los Angles, he headed toward San Francisco on Route 1.

The curving two-lane highway running between hills on one side and the Pacific Ocean on the other was one of the most beautiful drives in the world. This was the first time in my life I had seen such a sight. I hadn't even seen photographs as beautiful as this road was. We went slowly with Kirk coasting the jeep on downhill roads and it took the whole day to travel four hundred or so miles to Alameda, Kirk's parents' home.

The Wilsons lived in a house right on water. It reminded me of the houseboats in Kashmir I had read about. It was amazing to see the front door open to a road and the back door open to a dock with a boat in a slip. I stayed with the Wilsons for three days and got to know Kirk's dad, who liked to drink martinis and grill a steak on the dock. Kirk's mom was a very brisk and busy woman. She worked full-time at their business of making publicity signs and took care of the house as well. His two sisters, Joan and Karen, were still in school. It was a nice visit to an American family.

I had heard a lot about how beautiful Yosemite (I pronounced it "yo-say-mite," but Kirk insisted it was "yo-sem-a-tee") was and wanted to see it. Kirk said he couldn't go because he had a couple of job interviews. I decided to go alone by bus. I took Kirk's sleeping bag, my camera, and toothbrush in a backpack and Kirk dropped me off at the bus stop.

I managed to arrive in Yosemite without any problem. When I stood in line to get a space for camping, I learned that there was no camping space available for weeks. It was summer and the popular national park was booked solid. I stood there wondering what to do. A girl who was with her boyfriend was behind me in the line. She must have heard the clerk tell me there were no camping sites available. The girl gestured me to wait. After they had registered, they both came to me and the girl gestured again to follow them.

They were part of a large group of about thirty young men and women who were camping there for one week. She told me to put up my tent wherever I wanted. I didn't have a tent but told her that I would come back after sightseeing and join them. She tried to introduce me around, but most of the group were too stoned to pay attention. I was shocked to see that they were smoking pot openly and also drinking wine from huge jugs. They just smiled and stared into space. The young girl wrote on paper apologizing for the behavior of her friends. I told her it was all right and went out for a walk.

I spent the next two days walking the length and the breadth of the amazingly beautiful park. The Yosemite Falls and other smaller falls, the cliffs, especially El Capitan and the lake with its crystal clear, blue water were wonders of nature, the likes of which I had never seen. I thought of the beautiful places in Kashmir and the Himalayas. Perhaps they were equally or even more beautiful than the sights in Yosemite Park. However, reaching them would require months of trekking. Here in America, they had brought a highway right to the beauty of nature.

On the first night, I found an empty space away from the group and spread my sleeping bag on the rough ground and passed out. The next morning, I woke up to find all of them asleep. I found the public bathroom to do the morning ritual and bought some yogurt in the supermarket for breakfast. I spent the whole day visiting all of those beautiful places. At night, tired to the bone after all the climbing, I spread Kirk's sleeping bag again and was dead to the world in no time.

I woke up to bright flashing lights. I sat up, dazed, and saw several police cars parked next to our campsite and policemen standing surrounding four or five of my fellow campers. It appeared that they had a fight and the neighboring campers had called the police. I was wondering what to do when the young girl who had invited me to join the camp came over and wrote to me on a sheet of paper that she was sorry, but it would be better for me to go away as most of her friends were going to be arrested. She helped me pack my sleeping bag and gave me a parting hug and I walked out into the darkness.

It was only one in the morning and I had nowhere to go, but I wasn't interested in being arrested, either. So I started to walk toward the gate and finally got the first bus to Merced and took another bus back to Alameda. No more sharing of campsites, I told myself.

After spending about a week in California, I wanted to go back to Gallaudet and work. I had no money and asked Kirk if he knew anyone driving back to Washington, DC. He didn't. So the only way for me to return was to take a plane. I borrowed money enough to buy a ticket from Kirk's parents and flew back to Washington, DC.

It took me three weeks of full-time work to pay back Kirk's parents, but the trip was well worth it. I had some good photos and had met some very interesting people. I learned America wasn't all tall buildings and cowboys. It was full of wonders and one might need years and years to visit just some of them.

26

Other Adventures

EACH YEAR, I TRAVELED WITH ONE OR MORE FRIENDS OR even alone. The travels continued after Nirmala, my wife, arrived from India and later, after our children were born. I was able to visit all the states except for Alaska. Notable among those trips were a three-week jaunt with my friend Fred Orr, a Christmas trip to Florida with Dan and Gene, and several family vacations. However, narrating those trips would require a whole book, so I will share some anecdotes from those trips.

During the Christmas break of 1969, our friend Gene invited Dan and I to visit Miami for a few days. Gene's mother stayed there for the winter. We decided that Gene and I would ride the train to Miami and Dan, who had a car, would first go to visit his family in Indiana and then drive down to Miami to meet us and later we all would ride in his car back to Gallaudet.

This was my first ride in an American train. In India, trains are the main mode of travel. Only the very rich people traveled by air. When I was growing up in India, I traveled by trains, buses, oxcarts, and foot, but never by air. America is a country of cars and airplanes, I noticed. I loved trains, and the idea of riding a train for a thousand miles was exhilarating.

I told Gene I would ride third class because I didn't have enough money. He laughed and told me that, unlike India, there was no class system in American trains. Those who wanted a comfortable ride could rent a roomette. But the price for a roomette, Gene told me, was several times higher than the seat alone.

"Does it mean that I have to pay the same as someone who makes ten times more money than me?" I was puzzled.

"Yes and rub shoulders with those who make ten times more money than you." Gene thought it was a good thing. I would have preferred paying less and riding in a crowded compartment.

The American train I rode was so very different from the trains I had ridden in India. The seats were like those in airplanes, only larger and more comfortable. They were reserved for us. In India, except for in first class during those days, it was first come, first served. If you went to the bathroom, someone might stake claim for your seat. I looked forward to riding in comfort but wished there was a sleeper class, which is common in India.

"Forget sleeper class," admonished Gene. "That will cost three or four times more than this seat." So much for lack of class system in American trains, I thought.

We never really used our seats. There was a lounge with a snack bar where Gene and I spent the next fifteen hours. We drank coffee and beer and talked about world politics and made qualitative comments about passengers who passed us. One passenger especially got our attention.

A tall, lanky, and disheveled man, he held a beer bottle and his gait showed he had a few already. He would pass us and stop and shake hands with us each time he staggered by. After his third round, Gene began to take the initiative and would stand up whenever he saw him reel in and go forward and give him a special handshake. This handshake was elaborate. First you raise your hand at your side with the palm down, up to the head level, and then, after bending your knees like you were going to jump up, bring the hand down full force to meet the other guy's hand. Gene had to demonstrate it to the drunk guy first, with me as his partner. He was game and copied us, albeit awkwardly. I had no choice but to follow this charade. I tried to dissuade Gene, but he was having too much fun to stop that.

I wasn't ready for the warm weather in Miami. I knew it was warmer than Washington, DC, but I couldn't believe people were wearing shorts and golf shirts in December. The next morning, we saw women wearing bikinis sunning themselves. What a big change of weather in the same country.

Dan joined us the next day. Gene stayed with his mother and Dan and I took a room in the same building for a whopping $12 a night. Gene's mother, despite her old age, insisted on feeding us all meals. That reminded me of Indian culture. To keep her happy, we tried to eat at least one meal with her. We spent the days walking around on the beach and going to a greyhound racing track. We also met many deaf people, most of them from Canada. One Canadian deaf guy who was traveling with his whole family claimed he made a living by playing the horses. We went with him to dog races and I asked him if he minded my following his betting system. He didn't. So I began to bet on whatever dog he bet on. The only difference was that I was betting 10 percent of his bet. If he bet $10, I bet $1 and so forth. At the end of the evening, I was $3 richer and he was $30 richer, which was a decent amount of money in 1969 when the minimum wage was only $1.50 an hour.

The next evening, we decided to return. Just as we were leaving, Dan had an idea. "Why don't we go visit Key West?" Gene and I agreed. It was Dan's car, after all. We drove in the gathering darkness on an almost empty road. Sometimes, we could see the ocean on one side or the other. We made it to Key West just as the night was falling. It was a disappointment: a few closed stores and some empty bars. We drove south and then north on the street and headed back to Miami en route to Washington, DC. Dan drove all the way, since neither Gene nor I had a license. Dan had taught me how to drive and knew well enough not to let me touch the steering wheel. We arrived the next evening plowing through snow and sleet, which started to fall as we entered Virginia and wished we had stayed longer in Florida.

The cheapest trip I took was with Fred Orr. Fred was a classmate and a close friend. He was a good mechanic and helped everyone by changing their oil and performing minor tune-ups. Fred was a very methodical guy and there was no room for spontaneity when you were with him. He always bought gas at Sunoco and we always stayed in camps where our pup tent cost less than larger tents. We would drive a specific distance each day, visit the sites he had selected, and pitch our tent in a campsite he had picked. He would then get aluminum foil and make a small scoop and light charcoal for cooking. We would cook our dinner, which meant warming soup or beans and cold bread. Then we would go to sleep.

The next morning, we would eat cereal, make sandwiches for lunch, and hit the road again at a specific time. The routine was military-like, though Fred had never been in the military. He was just organized to a fault. We didn't spend even one night in a motel during the three-week trip, nor did we eat in a restaurant. We did, however, spend a few nights with friends. We also attended the wedding of Julie Munz and Chuck Theel, both of them our close friends. After the wedding in Kansas, we

traveled around and then stopped in Wisconsin where the wedding cel-
ebration had relocated.

During my senior year at Gallaudet, I became friends with Don Bangs. He
taught math at Gallaudet. Even though I was a student, we became close
friends. We discussed Ayn Rand and other contemporary writers. Don had
a lot of interests, but his major hobby was organizing trips to various places
for camping, rafting, skiing, and whatnot. These weekend trips helped
me learn water skiing, ice skating, and roller skating. However, learning
these sports when one is in his thirties and not very athletic is not easy. I
didn't break any bones but had a lot of bruises, sprains, and sore muscles.

However, before I go into Don's various trips, I need to share my
adventure in learning to snow ski. I never thought in my wildest dreams
that I would be able to ski. I learned to ski during my senior year. Our
senior class decided to have a skiing weekend in Pennsylvania. Skiing—
water or snow—was an alien concept to me. I had seen photos of people
skiing but never imagined myself being involved in those exotic sports.
However, I decided to take the plunge, literally, and asked Mineo, my

The charm of snow
never fades.

Japanese friend, if I could borrow his skis. He was an expert skier and his skis were top of the line.

Mineo looked uncomfortable. "Do you know the skis I have are top of the line and are designed for professionals?"

"I don't, but I guess having good skis will help me learn faster," I countered.

"No, you need smaller skis to learn. Later, when you become an expert, you can use skis like mine." Mineo was grasping for straws.

"OK, if you don't want to loan them to me, that's fine." I played the age-old dirty tricks and Mineo changed his mind.

He brought them to my room and taught me how tie the bindings and stand in the boots and gave me some pointers. The next morning, I loaded my skis in the bus. I was one of the few students who had his own skis and my skis were the focus on everyone's attention. Someone jokingly asked if I was an expert skier. Knowing well that he was aware about my total lack of experience, I told him, "Yes, I am." There were hidden smirks from onlookers.

It took me the whole day to finally stand up in my skis and not take two or three summersaults. Whoever watched me felt sorry for me and would whoosh to a stop with snow flying around them and give me pointers on how to stay in one place. However, those skis were tricky. They were, after all, top of the line, as Mineo had kept reminding. They were designed to glide over snow as fast as possible and not stop.

By the second day, with my whole body aching and bruises on my arms and legs, I could move down the easiest slope with one or two falls. This slope had a rope pull and so I didn't have to ride those scary chair lifts.

On the third day, I moved up to the more difficult slope, which required using a chair lift. Getting off the chair lift was a total disaster. I ended up sprawled on the snow with the skis up in the air. Two kindly fellows helped me to feet or the skis and guided me to a safe stop. After resting, praying, and cursing myself I took a bold step and found myself on my butt. From there, it was an ongoing struggle and took me half an hour to get down. But by then, I had developed more courage and confidence and went back to the chair lift for another round of self-abuse.

Skiing became a great hobby for me. I never missed the opportunity to ski. The last time I skied was in 1977, which was memorable for another reason.

Don had reserved a small house in Seven Springs in Pennsylvania. He insisted on calling it a chalet, however. This chalet was for four people, but eight were sharing to save money. Six of us taught at Kendall School. The three others were Don, who taught at Gallaudet, and Gordon, who taught with me at Kendall School, and his wife Laura. We drove Don's huge van for the trip, which seated two on seats and twenty on the floor like illegal immigrants. Don was the driver and, therefore, got one seat by default. The rest of us took turns at resting our butts in the coveted seat.

Before leaving, I decided to save money and asked Mrs. George, the mother of one of my students and who worked in the Kendall School cafeteria, to give me some sandwiches for the trip. She said she would do that and asked where and when I wanted the food. I told her the time and that I would pick up the sandwiches from the kitchen.

At 3:30, when we were to leave, Mrs. George stopped me. I had forgotten about the sandwiches. She said she would need two people to pick them up. I was puzzled and asked Gordon, my fellow teacher and old friend, to come with me to the cafeteria. There, to our surprise, was a large platter with about one hundred sandwiches and a huge six-gallon thermos jug of vegetable soup. I looked aghast as this was enough food to feed an army. Gordon gave me the "you did it again" look and could say nothing but "thank you" to Mrs. George. We put the large steel platter on my head like we carry weight in India and Gordon carried the six-gallon jug of soup to the parked van. The six other members of the skiing trip were standing in front of Don's van and glaring at the spectacle.

"What is this?" Don wasn't happy. "I do not have room for junk in my van." Gordon shrugged his shoulders and let me have the honor of explaining why we were carrying the whole cafeteria between us.

"We will need food. We got these chicken sandwiches and vegetable soup. These will be great for our trip and during our stay there," I blurted.

They all shook their heads in exasperation and moved around to make room for the platter and the thermos jug. Phil, who taught mathematics and had high standards about eating, wrinkled his nose and moved away from the food.

"We are not going to a desert," he said. "They have food where we are going."

Don laughed. "But this is free. Our taxes paid for it. You don't have to eat it." The matter was settled.

We skied for the weekend and had a lot of fun, but the main story was

the food. Five or six of us ate one or more sandwiches while Don was driving. Don asked for one and said it was delicious and followed up with a
second sandwich. At night, we some of us warmed the soup and ate it with
one or more sandwiches while others went out to some restaurant.

The chicken salad sandwich and vegetable soup became a conversation piece. We brought it up mainly to tease Phil. We would pick
up sandwiches and offer each other showing our cheap generosity for
laughs. The last thing I remember about the sandwiches was when I was
standing in the line for a chairlift, Don joined me. As we sat down on the
chairlift, Don looked at me and smiled.

"You hungry?" he asked mischievously.

Knowing Don and worrying that he might pull some stunt, I said no,
I wasn't hungry.

Then Don pulled his hand out of his ski parka and brought out yet
another chicken salad sandwich and we broke into a loud guffaw. People
in the chairs in front and back of us must have thought we were crazy.

Don, Gordon, and I had a lot of fun remembering chicken salad sandwiches and vegetable soup for a few months.

One summer, Don planned a Memorial Day camping trip for our group
of close friends, including Willis and Jackie who went with us for my first
experience in camping; Sue who taught at Kendall School and Elaine,
Don's friend in Deep Creek Lake. It is a beautiful place. We cooked, ate,
hiked and told jokes. On the second day, we got a bit bored and Willis,
who had grown up in Minnesota, suggested we rent a powerboat to water
ski. Most of them had some experience with water skiing. The closest to
water skiing I had come was watching movies of graceful men and women.
I knew I was not going to be graceful or skilled, but I was game to try. If I
could snow ski, I could water ski also!

All my wonderful friends wanted to make sure I learned how to ski.
Some of them demonstrated by going around one or two circles to show
how easy it was. It did look easy. You just stood there on the skis and
held the rope by handle and the boat pulled you. Great!

They helped me get into the skis and into the water where I sank
immediately. The water was cold and half the lake went into my nostrils
and mouth. I came up coughing and shaking my head. They tried to

suppress their laughter and help me get set up to try one more time. It happened again. I sank.

All I could do was fight to keep water out of my nose and curse myself for getting myself into this situation. Don, who had the "press box view" from the boat, explained that as the boat pulled away all he could see was my belly and knees splayed wide apart. I kept trying to rise up on the skis but was dragged in various acrobatic positions. All my "friends" had a great laugh.

The water was getting colder and I was shivering now. When I came up for breath, I tried to figure out how to control those skis. I also wondered why I had decided to make an ass of myself in Deep Creek Lake. I suddenly noticed that a couple of boats had stopped a few feet from where I was struggling and a man in one of the boats was filming me with his 8mm camera. Were my efforts at learning to ski that interesting? I looked around and noticed that Don and Willis were not looking at me anymore or rolling around on the deck. They had sheepish smiles and were looking elsewhere. I followed their gaze and saw that there was much more interesting phenomenon than an East Indian guy learning to ski: both of Sue's boobs had popped out of her string bikini while she was bending over trying to get her feet in the second set of skis. She wasn't aware of the attention she was getting or the reason for the congregation of boats around the dock. I suddenly understood where the adage "ignorance is bliss" came from.

When Sue finally learned about the "exposure" and saw the boats near the dock with cameras focused on her, she jumped, adjusted herself and walked back in a huff toward the camp. I stayed there while Don talked about seeing the "spectacle of seeing a man trying to give birth in a lake."

That was the end of my water skiing career.

27

My First Car

AMERICA IS A COUNTRY OF CARS. MY FRIEND DON USED to have a good laugh by comparing statistics about car ownership. He had learned that while there was one car for every three people in America, there was one car for every 1,100 people in India. I thought that was embarrassing, but to him it was hilarious.

I had never thought of owning a car. My goal was to finish my education and return to India to start teaching there and, hopefully, become the principal of a major school. This was a big dream and cars and other things didn't fit in it. If I was lucky, I might be able to buy a motorcycle for commuting.

However, I ended up buying a car. Or, rather, a car bought me.

I finished my coursework for my BA in three and a half years and applied to Gallaudet's graduate school. In those days, graduate school meant getting an MA in education or audiology. I was accepted at the end of my last undergraduate semester in the winter of 1970 but was told that I couldn't begin grad school until the fall of 1971. However, I could register for two graduate courses in addition to some undergraduate courses.

During the spring of 1971, while I took a hybrid program of graduate and undergraduate courses, I began to worry about money for graduate school. The grant from Gallaudet was to continue, but I would not have much time to work. So I began to look for another job. There was no job on campus available, so I extended my search off campus.

My Scottish friend Leslie and I both got a job entering data in a small company in Landover. Leslie had a car and we would ride together. We were allowed to work on the same shift. We agreed to work four hours daily in the evening. The data entry work was tedious. We had to sit in front of a machine and enter numbers using the numeric keypad. It was fine for an hour or so, but the monotony and boredom became unbearable after that. The nonstop moving of fingers reminded me of Charlie Chaplin's movie in which his character continues making the same motion even after he had finished work. On the second evening, Leslie and I were eating dinner in a small café and Leslie began to move his fingers on the table as if he were entering data on the numeric keypad. We both laughed at it, but then he became serious and said he was quitting.

"But how will I ride to work?" I asked him.

"That's your problem," said Leslie. "You have a lot of friends. Go ask them to drive you or borrow their cars." And that was that.

Not many of my friends had cars and after loaning me their car one or two times, they began to make excuses. They needed the car themselves or the car needed service. They began to suggest names of other people to borrow cars from. Within a week, I learned that if I continued to borrow cars from my friends, soon they would all be my former friends. So I thought about quitting the job or getting my own car.

The job was boring, but it paid more than my photography work at Gallaudet. There was also my pride. I didn't want to quit just because it was boring to let Leslie have a good laugh at me. I had managed to get my driver's license a year earlier. So I began to look for a car as my job depended on having a car. No car, no job. I had about $500 saved up and that was a decent amount in 1971.

I consulted with Mineo and Fred, two friends who fixed their own cars and discussed cars more than any other subject. Both of them were more than happy to help me find a car. Helen, a hearing graduate student who suffered from my car borrowing more than anyone else, volunteered to interpret when I went to check a car out.

Together we saw about five cars. Fred would test the car by driving it, checking oil and the machine, and getting under the car. We had agreed to buy a Volkswagen (VW) bug since it was the cheapest car and, according to Fred, the sturdiest. I liked its design and the fact that I had learned to drive in a VW owned by my roommate Dan helped with the decision. Learning to drive in Dan's brand new VW bug is another story, however.

Finally, we settled on a black VW bug. It was a 1965 vintage with fifty thousand miles on the speedometer. Fred, after driving it around, was satisfied. I went to the bank and took out $500 in cash and paid to the dealer the same day.

I was a proud owner of a car. I didn't have to beg my friends for rides to work. Instead, I began to offer rides to people I didn't know and who, after seeing my driving skills, decided not to take advantage of my generous offer. It was nice going out for a spin and the pride of ownership of a car is unparalleled. It is part of the Great American Dream.

Buying a car is one thing; maintaining it is another. I thought that paying $500 was the end of my expenses on the car and within three months, I would have paid the car off with the extra money I was making. Little did I know that expenses on a car start after you buy it, not end.

The car needed fixing. Fred volunteered to give it a free tune-up. But I had to buy parts and that cost money. The gas also cost money even though it was only twenty-nine cents a gallon at that time. Then, there was the insurance. I could not get a parking permit unless I had at least liability insurance. My hunt for insurance was another experience. They didn't sell insurance to new drivers, especially new deaf drivers. Finally, with the help of Willis, I found an insurance agent who sold me basic liability insurance for one year for a hefty $250. That was half the price of the car. I found out soon that the car that I had bought to keep my job had become a money pit. The car was not helping me to keep the job; I was working to keep the car.

I lost that car on my way to Deep Creek Lake where some of my friends were planning to camp. I had started to like camping thanks to Don who always found interesting places to camp. However, the main thing was being with friends. It was raining heavily and I could barely see the road. I braked too fast and too hard at a sharp curve and the car skidded. The car rolled a couple of times and I saw the world go round and round and thought I was going to die. I was going to become another statistic. A lot of people die in America in car accidents. However, the car finally stopped spinning and rested in a ditch with its roof on the ground. It was pretty hard to crawl out of the window. I stood in the pouring rain and looked at the black mass of a car and began to laugh.

That was the end of the car that I really loved and the job that I really hated.

28
Starting Graduate School

MY MAIN GOAL FOR COMING TO AMERICA WAS GETTING a degree that would allow me to teach deaf children. The BA degree in history and psychology had helped me prepare to get admission to Gallaudet's education department for an MA in deaf education. This was my ultimate dream: to become the first deaf Indian to hold this degree. I did some research and learned that only two Indian people—both hearing—had received this degree from Gallaudet. The Banerjees—father and son—had come to Gallaudet in 1892 and 1925 respectively. Both of them later became principals of the Calcutta School for the Deaf.

The graduate school at Gallaudet was housed in the Mary Thornberry (MT) Building, a beautifully designed, round building that housed both the education and audiology departments. It was an island on Gallaudet's campus. The undergraduate students went to the MT Building only to get their hearing aids fixed or for classes in communication. Otherwise, it was a hearing place as all audiology majors and most education majors were hearing. There were no deaf teachers in either department. Getting admission to both departments was not easy. Since Gallaudet offered a full scholarship through a government grant to all admitted students, the competition was pretty tight and the quality of students selected was high.

As a foreign student, I didn't qualify for the scholarship, but the grant from Gallaudet covered most of my expenses. I was sure that I could manage, despite the fact that visits to other schools for observations and work as teacher's aide was required and finally a whole semester for teaching that would curtail my part-time work.

There were only four deaf students among the thirty-five students. One of the deaf students, Mark, didn't know signs and could communicate using a telephone; therefore we didn't consider him deaf.

Pretty soon, I found out how different the graduate school was from the undergraduate. I thought I was going to sail through the graduate school. Wasn't I smart and didn't I make the dean's list all the time? However I was wrong. I got my first C in an hour-test in the curriculum development class and was shocked. I told my classmates that graduate school was hard. But they only laughed. All students from other universities said that the Gallaudet graduate school was not as hard as their undergraduate school.

This hit me hard. The BA program at Gallaudet didn't prepare us even for the Gallaudet graduate school. The tests and other assignments that got me an A or a high B in undergraduate school got me a low B or even C in graduate school. Some teachers were understanding and gave the deaf students higher grades than expected. But one teacher was firm and kept handing out Cs instead of understanding that we were in a different league. We Gallaudet students began to complain about discrimination against deaf students. Dr. Delgado, the dean of graduate school, who was always very sympathetic to deaf students, even held an inquiry. However, the professor came out clean when he submitted our work and compared it with the work of the other students. This "hearing" acted as a wake-up call to us. We began to study harder and apply ourselves. Soon we were competing with our hearing peers and doing better than some of them.

As I look back at my four years in Gallaudet's undergraduate school, I feel I wasted a lot of time sitting in classrooms. There were no challenges. The professors who challenged us—Dr. Schuchman, for example—had only four or five students in their classes. The teachers who let us sail had their classes full. All the students knew which teacher was "easy" and which one was "hard," and for some reason they picked the teachers that helped them sail through without doing much work.

One example of a teacher who had high expectations and forced us to think was Mr. Mio. He taught history. The problem with Mr. Mio was he signed very slowly. Despite being the football coach and also ice hockey coach where fluent communication was essential, he never really learned to sign well. I liked him because he was the first teacher I could understand well. This was not because of his signing skills but because of his lack thereof. He signed so slowly that I could understand him after a few months at Gallaudet. For students who signed fluently, he was equivalent of a sleeping pill. One could go to the bathroom and return before Mr. Mio had finished his sentence.

Almost all students complained that Mr. Mio was not a good teacher. I believed he was an excellent teacher. He challenged us and forced us to think. He didn't teach facts; he asked probing questions. Instead of just saying that there were three branches of government, he focused on how this checks-and-balances system worked and asked us if there was a better way. His forcing us to think didn't sit well with most students. It was the first time in my life I was being forced to think and I did balk in the beginning, but later I began to enjoy these discussions. I could not get enough of it and hung around with him after the class.

Mr. Mio left Gallaudet. Whether he was not awarded tenure or he left voluntarily is not clear. Most students were very happy at his leaving. Was it his signing skills or was it his demanding nature that caused his departure from Gallaudet? It will never be clear. However, Gallaudet is rife with teachers, even now, who can't sign well or understand students despite being there for decades. Most of them are not as demanding as Mr. Mio was.

Another teacher with a serious learning disability in signing had taught for over thirty years. He was considered a scholar in his subject area. Hard of hearing students or those who were skilled lipreaders mentioned how interesting and informative he was. However, the majority of students didn't understand one word he said or signed. He spelled in up and down jerky movement and someone trying to understand him only got seasick. His signing was worse than his spelling.

However, his classes were full. He had a wonderful system for grading. After each test or final exam, he would pass out the key, declare that he strongly believed in the honor system, and ask students to grade themselves. Needless to say, most of the students got an A+. Some graded themselves more honestly and got a B. This system worked for the teacher and the students. As for learning, that was limited to the teacher alone.

That teacher also had a heavy drinking problem. Everyone knew of it and talked about it, but no one apparently did anything about it. He was tenured as were several other professors who could not sign and didn't know how to teach.

There were good teachers, too. They cared for students. They signed well. However, they also suffered from the low expectation syndrome.

An idealistic teacher becomes cynical over time. Many of those teachers must have tried to raise standards and demand more from students only to see their efforts backfire in their faces.

As I look back, there were many bright students at Gallaudet who didn't work up to their potentials. They were pulled down by the majority of the students who unknowingly supported mediocrity and teachers who conformed to this demand.

29

Visiting India

EACH CHRISTMAS AND SUMMER, WHEN ALL GALLAUDET students began to pack their bags and leave for their homes, I felt homesick. Going to India cost more than I earned as a part-time photographer for six months. After paying for books and incidentals, there wasn't money left. I knew I would not be able to go home until I had finished my MA and that would be yet another one-way ticket.

But things happen! In October of 1971, an advertisement in the *Washington Post* jumped right at me. Air India was offering round-trip fares to India for $450. That was unbelievable. I had paid over $650 for a one-way trip to America in 1967. The round-trip fare was less than the one-way trip. It took me less than one minute to decide that I was going to India for the Christmas break!

The next step was saving money. I quit smoking and buying coffee and Coke from the vending machine and started working at the *Washington Post* on Saturday and Wednesday nights. Then I wrote to Nirmala about my plans to come to India and asked her not to tell anyone. It would be a surprise for everyone. However, I also told my nephew Surinder, who had moved to America a few months earlier, about it. Thus, by the time I arrived in India, everybody knew about it. The secret of keeping secrets is to tell one or two persons, asking them to keep it a secret.

I didn't think of other expenses related to going to India. The fare was from New York City. I had to find a way to go to NYC and back. One does not go home after more than four years without some gifts. All of this was going to cost money. The original budget of $450 swelled to $700 even after cutting corners. So I decided to dig into my rainy day deposit of a few hundred dollars.

Don Bangs resolved the problem of the trip to New York City. He was going home to visit his parents (so was I) and offered to drop me off at Kennedy Airport on "his way" to his parents' home. He didn't tell me that his parents' home was in upstate New York and New York City wasn't exactly on "his way home."

That trip to India proved to be an odyssey in itself. It was the first time I was going to fly in a jumbo jet—a Boeing 747. The idea of flying in a machine with more than four hundred people was gripping in itself. Little did I know that this trip would be very exciting for other reasons.

The line for the plane—the coveted Boeing 747—was really long. That made me wish for a smaller plane. The interesting thing about this line was that everyone in it was Indian like me. During my four-plus years in Washington, DC, I had seen, perhaps, ten people from India. Seeing this huge number in one place was surprising. I knew I wasn't the only person from India in the United States.

As I stood behind a lot of people in the line, suddenly the line broke off. I tried to ask fellow passengers. They just told me to follow them. The plane was several hours late!

That was the month when East Pakistan decided to secede from West Pakistan and the war, later known as the Bangladesh Liberation War, was raging. It appeared that some threats of sabotaging the plane were made and all Indian planes were being checked for security reasons.

I learned about this later. At that time, all I knew was the plane was late. We were herded to a restaurant for dinner. I sat with a group of my countrymen around a round table. All of them were talking with each other animatedly. I had no idea what they were talking about but wanted to join them. Being at Gallaudet for a long time had conformed me to be a part of conversations. These people didn't know signs, but they could write. I thought it would be a good idea to introduce myself as a first step.

Since they were all talking and butting in would have been very rude, I took a newspaper and wrote on its margin, "My name is Madan Vasishta, I am working on my MA at Gallaudet College." I pushed to the guy sitting next to me, as he looked pretty nice. He had thick spectacles and look like a scholar and a kind person. He took the newspaper from my hand, read my note, and wrote under it, "My name is Dr. Sharma. I teach people who are working on their PhDs." He finished his notes with a flourish and almost breaking the pen and pushed the newspaper toward me as a dismissal. That was pretty humiliating. After that I didn't try to be a part of any conversations.

The plane left three hours late from Kennedy. We had to change planes in London. I learned that the connecting flight had already left and we were to wait for the next flight. The "next flight" was "in a few hours" but these "few hours" kept stretching. We walked around in the airport. Heathrow was very small then and there wasn't much space to walk around.

I had no idea was what going on, so I kept asking the Air India staff, but they weren't helpful. I was worried if I took a nap or wasn't paying attention, the plane might leave without me. One guy, who must have seen my frustrations, came over to me and wrote on the margin of the magazine he was reading that "no one really knows how long it will take. I will tell you when we are ready to leave." He told me he was a professor at Penn State. We talked a bit about deafness as he taught a course in special education. He didn't understand why I couldn't lipread. He had a strong belief that lipreading was tied to intelligence.

Later in the evening, we were herded in buses to a hotel nearby. I just followed other passengers. By this time, I could recognize every one of the four-hundred-plus people and kept them in my sight to follow them wherever they went. However, now I just stayed close to the special education professor. He would introduce me to whomever he was talking to. People looked wary of me. It was obvious they didn't like a deaf man flying with them.

The next day, we were brought in a hurry for a "waiting plane." Instead, it was us who ended up waiting for a plane. Finally, after almost thirty-six hours, we got on a plane for Bombay, instead of Delhi where I was supposed to go. I had to then spend another twelve hours at Bombay airport for the connecting flight to Delhi.

The arrival at Bombay airport for me proved to be a shock. I was visiting India after four and half years. I also had spent twenty-six years of my life there. However, I felt like a foreigner. I had forgotten or had blocked out what life in India was like.

Instead of the overly polite immigration person at Dulles, I had to fend with the extremely rude khaki-clad subinspector in Bombay. He took my passport as if it were dirty, thumbed through it for an eternity looking for something that didn't exist. Then, with an expression of disgust, he stamped it hard and threw it at me. This wasn't the welcome I was ready for.

The customs officials were a bit polite but also thorough. They opened my suitcase and handbag and went through everything as if it was their own bag. The tape recorder, a hot item in India at that time, was examined and discussed by three people. They told me I had to pay custom duty on it. I told them that it was under the allowable limit for importing tax-free. They didn't agree with me. Finally, I knew why they were polite. One of them scribbled a dollar sign on the margin of the note. I took out a five dollar bill, tucked it in my palm, and shook hands with one of them. I was then cleared. They helped me pack the bag, albeit in a messy way. I knew then that I was back in India.

There were other shocks waiting for me. A throng of people was attached to a steel rod fence with their hands stuck in, and it seemed they were yelling at us for something. I asked the special education professor what they wanted. He took out a dollar bill from his wallet and put his thumb under his index finger and flicked it. That was the common Indian gesture for rupee. Then he wrote "black." The crowd of over one hundred people on the other side of the fence was asking for dollars at twice the official exchange rate.

Communication in those days was by telephone only and I had no way to telling my family that I would be late by days, not hours. I wasn't aware that while I was waiting for the plane to get ready, my family and friends were also waiting for me to arrive. My brother-in-law, B. K. Sharma, whom we called Jijaji and who worked for Air India, managed to check the passenger list from New York. It seemed that even the airline wasn't giving correct information. About fifty of my relatives and friends had come to the airport twice with marigold garlands to welcome me back to India. They had to wait and wait and then go back home.

Somehow, Jijaji found out that our plane was diverted to Bombay. He let my elder brother Narain know, who called a family friend, a doctor who practiced in India whom I had never met, to meet me at the airport. He found me after asking different people and introduced himself. I knew his name and was impressed that such an important person had come to see me. He spent a few hours with me, bought me some food, and tried to talk to me by writing on a paper. He took my hand and held it while we walked around. This is a common practice in India, but after my long stay in America, I wasn't used to a man holding my hand. I felt uncomfortable but didn't say anything. I rebuked myself for becoming too American and reminded myself how an American guy had slapped my hand after I had put my hand on his forearm.

Finally, I arrived in Delhi to a crowd of smiling relatives and friends. Nirmala, my wife, was here too. However, her face was hidden behind a veil. I could feel her looking at me through the thin material, but I couldn't see her. She had come to Delhi along with my mother. She had been living with my parents all of this time.

Both my brothers and friends hugged me hard. I went limp first and then remembering my roots, hugged back. My deaf friends, Suraj and Kesh among others, came forward and asked how I was. I responded only to see puzzled looks on their faces. I didn't realize that I was using ASL. I had forgotten Indian Sign Language.

I spoke Hindi and Punjabi without any problem as I had used those all my life and had the opportunity for using these with Indian people I met and also with Surinder, my nephew, who had moved to America in the summer of 1971. However, I had learned ISL when I was twenty years old and had not used it for more than four years. I had to relearn it. It took me a few hours with Kesh and other friends to be able to comfortably sign in ISL.

With Nirmala in 1971 visiting Lohara.

I forgot to mention that I had shoulder length hair and the first thing
Narain Bhaiji did was to send me to a barber with Mahesh, my cousin,
who could sign pretty well. Bhaiji didn't think it was a good idea to go to
Gagret, our village, with long hair. Babuji might disapprove.

After spending two days visiting friends, we all went to Gagret. Babuji
had been waiting for me and had sent a telegram to Bhaiji asking him to
bring me to Gagret. About fifteen of us traveled by train to arrive the next
morning in Gagret. I remember it like it was yesterday, getting off the bus
and then walking with Bhaiji, Narain, and Sham toward the shop where
Babuji held his court on a daily basis. But the word had gotten to Babuji
through someone and he was coming with Vaid Niranjan, his best friend
and the ayurvedic doctor who had tried to cure my deafness. We met
half-way to his shop. I touched his feet and he blessed me then. I moved
behind him as he started to walk. There were about twenty of us walking
behind him and people gathered around watching us. It was like a parade
for a few hundred yards until the bazaar ended.

I wasn't aware that Babuji had planned a *yagna*—open kitchen and
worship service—to celebrate my return. He had not fattened any calf;

The first visit to India with deaf friends.

instead there were several hours of chanting and *puja* in front of a cere-monial fire. I had to sit through it. This was to purify my sins that I might have committed while living abroad. I was glad that I was a Hindu and the sins were being forgiven by chanting mantras. If I were a Catholic I would have had to say a few thousand Hail Marys among other penances.

The *yagna* lasted all day and I met over one thousand people from several villages who had come to see me. Babuji must have spent a for-tune in feeding them all and he looked very pleased. He had prospered during the time I was in America as the resin extraction business he had started, which had been losing money, finally took off.

After about ten days in Gagret, I returned to Delhi to visit with my deaf friends. As we were waiting for the bus at the bus stop, a well-dressed guy came over to me after to talk to Babuji. He was a travel agent and wanted to know if I had some dollars to exchange. I did. He paid me four hundred rupees for a $20 bill. The official rate of exchange would have gotten me only 150 rupees. He made this exchange right in public and later had a hard time retrieving the $20 bill, as everyone around wanted to see what the American money looked like.

I got into the bus and looked outside at Babuji, who was talking to Vaid Niranjan. They were deep in discussion. The bus slowly moved and I waved to him. I didn't know this was the last time I was going to see him. He was stoic and had never told me he loved me and never men-tioned that he was proud of me. But he didn't have to do that. His strong and solid personality, his silent gaze, and his touch on my head when he blessed me said it all and very eloquently.

It was hard to leave Nirmala alone again. But it was harder to leave Babuji. My mother, whom we all called Bhabhi, had the talent of becom-ing a part of the background, and even though I missed her, her absence was easier to tolerate.

Nirmala was upset. She asked me to take her with me or I should stay in India. I told her angrily that my staying in India was out of the ques-tion. I had to finish my MA. And taking her with me was impossible, as I had no means of support except the scholarship and the part-time job. I told her that the worst was over. Only a little more than a year was left and almost five years were gone. "Almost five years" sounded more impressive than "a bit over four years."

I forgot that time flew for me with my full load of studies, a job, and all the extracurricular activities. For Nirmala, it was a pure grind of cooking and cleaning and taking care of my parents. I began to understand the difference in our situation. However, there was no choice. Living off campus would have meant renting an apartment and paying for all food and maintenance expenses. All of these were beyond my means.

We returned to Delhi where my deaf friends were waiting. I visited the All India Federation of the Deaf and attended several public and private dinners sponsored by Delhi Deaf Association and friends. These daily dinners became a drag and tiring. One thing I learned slowly that everyone was disappointed that I had not brought gifts for them. There were so many things that were common in America that were rare or unavailable in India. Hot items were the audio tape recorders, nylon saris, lipstick, razor blades, cameras, films, and so forth. I did want to get those gifts but was able to afford only for close family members. It wasn't only the question of money but also of baggage limitation as well as strict custom rules.

Several of my old hearing friends started to talk with me even though they knew signs. They were very disappointed that I couldn't lipread after my four years of education in America. This belief that education helps lipreading was further strengthened by a movie, *Koshish*, which was released a year earlier. It was a love story, but the hero who is totally deaf goes to the United States and upon his return speaks perfectly and lipreads better than hearing people can hear.

I was a disappointment in many ways! I was also disappointed. Old friends with whom I could chat for hours appeared to become a drag after a few minutes. The things they talked about were the same things we used to discuss before I went to America. I realized that the four years spent at Gallaudet had changed me. I had new friends and new interests.

The most irritating part was the limited communication I had with my family and hearing friends. I was used to it before I went to America. That was the norm. Now, after four years of a rich communication environment, I was spoiled. I didn't like sitting in a group for hours and smiling when everyone was smiling and pretending to be happy and contented. In sum, I longed for Gallaudet.

I learned you couldn't go back home again.

30

Plans to Return to India

DURING THE SPRING OF 1973, I APPROACHED DR. DELgado, the dean of the graduate school, and explained my plans to work in India as a consultant or principal of a school for the deaf. I felt that with my MA from Gallaudet and observing for six years what was going on here, I would be a great resource for educators of deaf in India. Delgado added that more than that I would be a great role model for deaf people in India. Even in America, he said, there were few deaf people who had a master's degree. I was, perhaps, the only deaf person from India who had a master's degree in deaf education.

We discussed various angles and came to the conclusion that we needed to get support from the Indian embassy. He had his secretary call the embassy and set up an appointment for us to meet someone with a fancy title of "minister of education." He was responsible for coordinating educational opportunities in India and helping Indian students in America.

Dr. Delgado and I met him in his office in the embassy. He was a very nice guy—very diplomatic and appropriate. He listened to Dr. Delgado explaining about Gallaudet College and my MA degree and how I could be of great asset to deaf people in India. The minister watched Delgado, and I could see his discomfort at Delgado's signing while talking to him. He raised his hand very politely and asked Delgado (who kept interpreting for me) what he was doing with his hands. Delgado explained that he was signing for me so I would know what they both were saying. The minister first looked mystified and then smiled in understanding. He asked why I couldn't lipread and Delgado let me explain it to him. I told him that lipreading was more like an art than a skill. Some people were lipreaders and some not. This seemed to satisfy him.

We left with the agreement that I would write application letters to the 122 schools for the deaf listed in the directory published by the All India

Federation of the Deaf and the embassy would mail those in the "diplomatic pouch."

A week later, with the help of Dr. Delgado's secretary, I had 122 letters typed and ready for mailing. She typed one letter without an address and made the required number of copies then typed in the address of each school listed in the directory. I carried the big bundle to the embassy and personally delivered it to the minister. I noticed the change in his behavior. He was very polite to me when in company with Dr. Delgado. Now, when seeing him alone, he didn't respond to my questions like "How much time will it take for these letters to arrive in India?" He even refused to take the bundle of letters from me when I tried to hand those over to him. Instead, he raised his hands with palms facing me to tell me to hold. Then he called a peon and then signaled me to give it to the underling. I felt embarrassed by this act of humiliation but kept smiling.

That was in March and I hoped that by mid-April I was going to have a few offers. I was more qualified than most of the principals in schools for the deaf in India, I told myself, therefore, I should be getting many offers to teach. Maybe they would offer a higher salary since I was educated in America. Maybe they would offer an administrative position.

I waited for months. There wasn't a single job offer from India. Not

Graduation parade in 1971.

even for teaching. I asked Dr. Delgado's secretary to call the embassy. They told her that the applications were mailed out as agreed. They told her to tell me to wait.

I was getting worried about what to do in the fall. I didn't want to fly to India without a job offer in my hand. Kirk and other friends kept encouraging me to apply for a job at Kendall School and other schools just to be safe. I did that and got three offers—one in Canada, one in Michigan, and one right on Gallaudet's campus at Kendall School. I decided on Kendall School.

As the time for graduation came closer, friends and acquaintances began to ask me on a daily basis when I was going to India. I would tell them a general date based on my assumption about getting a job in India. However, this constant questioning was becoming pretty irritating. I knew they meant well and when someone asked me the question, he or she wasn't aware that I had already answered that question eleven times that day. After that job offer from Kendall School, I could tell them I was going the next year. Some of them laughed. "We have heard of this 'next year' promise from many people." I didn't like this ridicule and told myself that I will show them next year when I pack my bags and buy a one-way ticket back to India.

31
Challenges in Teaching

HAVING A PRESTIGIOUS MASTER'S DEGREE FROM GALLAU-
det assured me of a good job and also provided me with the tools to teach
effectively, not necessarily in that order. I was full of confidence and was
sure that I was going to become a great teacher and change the lives of
students that passed through my classroom. Me and millions of other
young teachers!

The students at Kendall Demonstration Elementary School (KDES),
as it was known then, weren't the kind of students any of the professors in our department had taught or even knew. The curriculum was
geared for teaching the average middle-class white American deaf student. Almost all of our students came from the northeast neighborhoods
in Washington, DC. Almost all the students were from families on government assistance. None of these students' parents had received any
support or guidance in parenting a deaf child. Most of our students didn't
have access to preschool. They started school late—when they were six,
seven, or even ten years old. They had no spoken or signed language and
depended on gestures to communicate.

I was assigned to the middle school. There were twenty students—all
age fourteen to fifteen—and five teachers. All of us, except for Dennis
Cokely, were deaf. However, Dennis was also the most skilled signer of
"Kendalese," the term he had coined for the variety of gestures used by
our students. Jackie Mann was our part-time supervisor. She taught one
or two classes. Gordon Bergan taught arithmetic, reading was Marianne's
area, Dennis had communication, and I was to teach social studies.

The five of us worked very well together. Jackie was more of a col-
league than a supervisor. She gave us full rein to do our job, which we did
by flying by the seat of our pants.

There was no curriculum to speak of and we had to do "our own

Playing Santa Claus in a Christmas play at Kendall School.

thing." After meeting with the students, I knew following a formal social studies curriculum or using a textbook was out of question. None of the students could read and some couldn't even spell their names correctly. I talked to some teachers who had worked with this group and learned that they had been in school for five to seven years. Why they weren't able to spell even three-letter words correctly was a mystery to me.

I put my photography skill to work and prepared a montage of class members with their names under each photograph. Their job was to learn to spell names of each classmate and teachers. I thought I'd be able to do that in one or two days, but after a full week, I found myself where I'd started. One student kept spelling egg as G-E-E even after a full week of practice.

All the students were of normal intelligence but they hadn't been exposed to language when they were younger. When they were babies and toddlers, when their hearing peers were learning a spoken language, these children were just staring at moving lips and trying to decipher ambiguous gestures made by their parents and siblings. This didn't help them develop a meaningful language—spoken or signed. Trying to teach them how to spell at the age of fifteen was like trying to teach someone to sprint who had never learned to walk. They tripped over letters.

Two weeks later, with limited success in my efforts to teach them to spell each other's names, I realized that there were more important things that they need to learn: they needed to learn how to protect themselves.

We teachers had a continental breakfast with students every morning. During that time, we had good conversations. The students told us about what was going in their neighborhoods, which was very educational for us. One day, a student showed me a crumpled slip of a paper. He had written on it "High Voltage." He asked me what it meant. I explained and then asked him where he had seen the words. He told me it was around the corner from his house. He was playing there and a man had pulled him away pointing at that word. The student didn't understand what those words meant. I explained to him how electricity can kill and why the man was so insistent that he not play there.

I had an idea! I spent a few hours going through the card catalog of the school library and found, among other things, signs for fifty-two danger words. These included "high voltage," "railroad crossing," "danger," "poison," and others. First, I had my students copy the words, then they all took turns acting out the words, and finally, we made a videotape, showing each phrase in English, the signs for those phrases, and then the students acting out each phrase. All of this took about three weeks and all the students finally recognized the danger vocabulary. However, they still couldn't spell even one of the words. I gave up. The goal, after all, was to avoid eating poison. They still would be able protect themselves without spelling the words.

The progress was slow but steady. The students learned more about life while talking with us during breakfast, lunch, and recess. They enjoyed stories from history, which I told in signs. They were insatiably curious and asked really good questions. Slowly I realized that they could learn as long as they weren't required to memorize spelling or write sentences. Learning can happen in many forms, and, in their cases, it was through rich two-way communication.

.

32

Nirmala's Arrival

IN THE SUMMER OF 1973, I STARTED TEACHING SOCIAL studies at Kendall School in its middle school department. Now that I was gainfully employed and wasn't going back to India right away, I decided to bring Nirmala to America for a year and return to India in 1974 with her. I bought a ticket for her with my savings and sent it to Babuji along with a copy of the letter from Kendall School, so that Nirmala could get a visa.

However, it took two months before she could join me. Bhai Narain sent me a letter indicating the date and flight number of her arrival. Since changing planes in New York to Washington, DC, would not be easy for her, I decided to drive up to New York to meet her. My nephew Surinder, who had moved to America two years earlier, decided to ride with me. He knew an Indian family who lived in New York, and we were to spend the night with them.

Kirk and Annette, his new wife, were living in Boston at that time. They decided to drive over to New York to join me to for Nirmala's arrival. I was worried about her getting a huge cultural shock. I had read hundreds of books related to America and seen all of those American movies before coming here and still had to go through experiences that dropped jaws—sometime mine but mostly of my American hosts. Nirmala, on the other hand, was coming straight from a little village. She had no acquaintance with John Wayne or Zane Grey. At least, I thought, she would not be looking for cowboys and Indians.

Surinder and I stayed with a Mr. Sharma, Surinder's friend, who lived in Queens. He and some members of his family also decided to join us to meet Nirmala at the airport. Thus, we had six or seven of us to welcome her to America. I was happy comparing this small entourage to my own arrival with no one there.

Annette had the foresight to have Kirk buy some flowers. "Women like flowers," she told us. I recalled buying a small jasmine garland for Nirmala in Delhi, the kind women put around their hair bun. That was the extent of flower giving. I was worried that she might throw the flowers away after getting them. I was wrong. Women do love flowers.

The Air India plane was full of Indian people and finding her among more than three hundred people walking out of the immigration gate wasn't easy. Kirk kept teasing me, "I hope you can recognize your own wife."

I didn't know how I was going to greet her. I thought of how American couples meet after two years or even after a few days. There is the tight hug and a long kiss. The couple separate when they realize that they are in a public place, put their arms around each other, and walk away talking to one another.

Annette was curious about the Indian culture. "Will you kiss her? Hug her? Make her feel good and welcome," she kept reminding me. Kirk said, "Madan is worried about recognizing his wife and Indian culture forbids public demonstration of affection." While this deep cultural discussion was going on, Surinder and I, the two people who knew what Nirmala looked like, kept searching the faces of the throngs of the Indian people coming toward us loaded with handbags.

Finally, I saw her. She walked slowly with a small bag in her hand. She wasn't looking for anyone, rather at the floor—like a typical Indian new bride arriving in her in-laws' house. The fact that this "house" was a huge country was another matter and none of us thought about that.

None of us knew what to do. It was a novel situation for all of us. Surinder had the easiest role. He went forward and touched her feet as required of younger people to show respect to their elders. Nirmala gave a shy smile and began to talk to him. This broke the ice and Kirk came forward with the flowers he had been carrying dutifully. Nirmala took them and held them in her hand and began to take stock of who was there. I had to go forward and touch her shoulder as I couldn't think of anything else. This action would have been taboo in India and I had taken advantage of the American "permissiveness."

I introduced Nirmala to Kirk and Annette. "Friends," I said of them. Then I introduced her to Mr. Sharma and his son: "Surinder's father's friend and his son." She didn't say anything. While we all stood there awkwardly, Kirk had a great idea. "Let's go to the car." Everyone was happy that the spell was broken. We walked slowly as a group. Surinder talked with Nirmala and I talked to Annette while Kirk talked to Mr. Sharma. We got into the two cars and drove to Mr. Sharma's apartment in Queens. Nirmala, as always happened in an Indian family, disappeared with the women, except for Annette, who was stuck with us men.

The next day, Nirmala, Surinder, and I drove back to Arlington to the apartment I had rented. This was a new experience for both of us. This was the first time she was living with her husband, not with the whole extended family. She was excited and started to learn about American living.

I decided to first introduce her to my friends, especially Chuck and Margie. Margie taught at Gallaudet and when she learned that Nirmala was coming, she decided to learn Hindi. We thought she was kidding, but she was serious. In the 1970s, there was little or no interest in learning Hindi and there were no classes. But Margie checked around and found that the Georgetown University offered Hindi classes for diplomats. She couldn't attend those classes but was able to find a few books on beginning Hindi in the university bookstore. Learning a new language is very hard and learning it from a book is much harder. I tried to dissuade her, but she was adamant and took it as a challenge.

She amazed me, as within a few weeks she not only had read the Devnagari alphabet used to write Hindi and Sanskrit but was also writing it. She showed me simple sentences she had written in her neat hand, and I had nothing but praise for her hard work.

Chuck thought she was nuts. He told her that when people immigrate to America, the great melting pot, they learned English. Americans didn't learn their language. But for Margie, learning Hindi had become a pure hobby by now and she was spending all her free time on it. Chuck decided he also needed to learn some basic vocabulary, which in Chuck's parlance meant expletives. I was happy to oblige. I explained how these short sentences were similar to some very common American utterances establishing rather close physical relationships between siblings and mother and son. He really enjoyed speaking those words and began to use them on people in the street who annoyed him by walking slowly or for whatever reason. He felt very good. Learning a new language is very beneficial, he declared.

The main reason for taking Nirmala to Chuck and Margie's home first wasn't just because they were my closest friends at that time but also because I thought Nirmala would enjoy communicating in Hindi with an American woman.

We drove to their apartment, which was only about a ten-minute drive from Arlington. Nirmala was, of course, shy as she was meeting new people in a new country. However, Chuck and Margie were also very self-conscious. It was an awkward situation. They didn't know Hindi and Nirmala didn't know signs or even English. I had to act as the interpreter. I translated Chuck and Margie's questions into Hindi and Nirmala would respond by tracing it on her palm in Hindi, which I would then sign to Chuck and Margie.

This was very cumbersome and the already awkward situation became even worse. Then I remembered Margie's Hindi and asked her to write something to Nirmala. Margie first tried to avoid it as she didn't have the confidence yet to use her limited knowledge of Hindi for real-world communication. But Chuck and I encouraged her. Finally, Margie wrote in clear Hindi, "*Aap kaisi hain? America ko swagat.*" (How are you? Welcome to America.) Nirmala read it with great joy and wrote below it, "*Bahenji, main aap se aur aap ke pati se mil kar khush hun. Aap meri pati ke mitter hain. Main aap ki bahut abhari hun.*" (Dear Sister, I am very happy to meet you and your husband. You are both my husband's friends and I am thankful to you.)

Margie couldn't read it. It was beyond her level, but also she had no experience reading handwritten Hindi. She was lost and looked embarrassed. So I translated the text to her and Chuck. Then we all sat there smiling and wondering what to do. Margie suggested that we drink tea. She had learned about the Indian custom of offering tea to visitors. Nirmala following the Indian custom, said no. She didn't want tea. I explained to Nirmala that in America if you say no, they won't offer it to you again. In India, the host will keep insisting until the guest agrees to go ahead and drink tea or have food. I also had to explain to Chuck and Margie that Nirmala's "no" was just a formality and, yes, we will drink tea.

We spent an hour with Chuck and Margie, but the awkwardness of the situation made it seem like many hours. This was also the first and the last time Margie used Hindi with Nirmala. The effort was great and results meager. As time passed, Nirmala learned English and also American Sign Language. Margie began to lose interest in her Hindi learning and what she had learned, she forgot in a few months. Chuck had his last laugh.

33

Setting Up Home

I HAD MANAGED TO PURCHASE A SOFA AND A DINING table with five chairs. I was also a proud owner of a desk—an unfinished door panel lying on two steel drawers. I also had a foam mattress lying on the floor. That was our bed. This was the sum total of our furniture. Needless to say, Nirmala was disappointed.

She had waited for six years in India while her husband finished his studies and had gotten a nice job. My American salary was princely from Indian standards and she had been listening to everyone in India about the nice life she was going to have only to find a mattress on the floor for a bed. She was horrified when she saw it. The furniture didn't impress her. Worse than the furniture was the lack of enough pots and pans. The pots and pans I had salvaged from Kirk's apartment were all right for cooking American food, but there was no "*tawa*" (a heavy griddle) or rolling pin for making chapatis. There were no Indian spices. There wasn't anything in the refrigerator except for a case of half-finished beer. The pantry had a bottle of Scotch and a bottle of gin. I lived a simple life.

The next morning, I took Nirmala to the Safeway to buy groceries. Rajesh, a friend from India who shared an apartment with Surinder, accompanied us. Since we had nothing to eat, we decided to arrive at the Safeway when it opened at eight in the morning. However, it was still closed. We sat down outside the Safeway and waited. However, after fifteen minutes, the store was still closed. Nirmala didn't mind. In India, stores closed and opened whenever the owner wanted to. She wasn't aware that American stores, especially large chains like Safeway, were not even a minute late.

We saw other people come, park their cars, and loiter around. Rajesh asked one man and learned that it was the first day of daylight saving time. In the fall, the clock was moved back. I had forgotten it, as had

Rajesh. We had to explain to Nirmala this strange American custom of moving the clock twice a year. She didn't understand the rationale for it. Her first American shopping experience wasn't very pleasant.

Slowly, we began to establish our household. Nirmala liked to work. She cleaned the apartment daily and kept it spotlessly clean. I told her not to waste her time and to focus on learning English. But as a proud housewife, she was focusing on her house. English could wait.

I taught her how to use the washer and dryer in the basement of our apartment building. She liked the idea of a machine doing the washing but wasn't very satisfied with the washer. I learned later that she used the broom handle in the washer to make sure the clothes were fully rinsed. Everything must be perfectly clean for her and it was irritating to me.

Soon, like all good wives, she began to find flaws in the décor and my way of living. My favorite pair of jeans with patches ironed on both knees disappeared after one week of her arrival. When I asked, she said innocently that she had thrown it in the trash.

I was livid. "You mean you threw out my new pair of jeans?"

"Not new, the one with the patches on its knees. Only *chamars* [untouchables] wear patched clothes. How could you wear tattered jeans?"

My explanation that it was a new pair and I had bought the patches separately and had ironed them on only confused her. Why would one make a new pair of jeans old and patched? I would have asked the same question six years earlier, I thought, and gave up.

She didn't like the mattress on the floor. My explanation that we were living here only for one year and then moving back to India didn't sound logical to her. She wanted a real bed. The windows needed curtains and the table lamps needed tables to put under them. I promised her that slowly, we would buy these pieces of furniture from other people. She couldn't believe that I was going to buy used furniture and was horrified when she learned that I had bought the dining table and chairs for $25 from my friend Sue when she upgraded her dining room. A good Brahman didn't buy used furniture, even from friends. I knew that, but I had lived in America for six years and it didn't bother me.

She was very resourceful, however. She covered two empty cardboard boxes with a flowery Indian bed sheet and put them under the lamps. They looked pretty good as tables. Then she used two other bed sheets she had brought with her to make curtains. The trunk in which I used to stash all my junk during summers and stored in the basement of the dormitory was also covered by another colorful bed sheet now and was an elegant television stand.

My friend Donnie, who taught at Kendall School with me, told me about houseplants. He suggested I should have plants in my apartment as they cleaned air and were beautiful and good for mental health. I thought plants, cats, and dogs were for other people—not me. But Donnie suggested that Nirmala might like them. To humor him, I took the few small cuttings he had brought from his house. He explained how each of these would grow roots and should be planted separately in small pots. I took the jar home and explained to Nirmala, thinking she was going to put these roots in the same place she had put my patched jeans. However, she didn't. A few days later, she wanted to show me something. She had six very healthy plants growing in jars and other makeshift "pots." She was disappointed that I had not noticed her hard work. She had gone out, dug out good dirt from under some trees, and lovingly planted those little stems Donnie had given me. She has a green thumb and anything she touched grew. On the other hand, any plant I touched withered. Soon the number of plants grew and grew fast. I still didn't notice them and she had to point those out to me.

Many years later, when we were living in Texas and Nirmala and our daughter Neerja had gone to India while our son Dheeraj and I stayed at home in the states, Nirmala called Dheeraj. After the usual preliminaries, she asked him how the plants were doing.

"Daddy, mom wants to know how the plants are doing," he interpreted.

"Plants? Do we have plants?" I asked.

Dheeraj made the mistake of repeating my question to his mom and then had to move the receiver away from his ear very fast.

Nirmala, for good reason, was livid. She lad left explicit instructions for watering the plants—the location of each plant and amount and frequency for watering. I had overlooked that part of instructions.

"Tell her we will take care of the plants." I wanted to her to calm down. After Dheeraj hung up the phone, we both walked around the house. There were about fifty plants hanging from the ceiling and sitting on tables and the floor. Both of us watered all of them. Our efforts were half-hearted and even the plants knew we both were "brown thumbs."

Nirmala returned in three weeks. Half her plants were dead and the other half were ready to commit suicide. She wasn't very happy.

34

Acculturating Nirmala

I HAD A HARD TIME LEARNING ABOUT AMERICA. I DIDN'T want Nirmala to have any problems and began to explain to her about the "American way of life." However, my six years here had jaded me and many things that had shocked me and were going to shock Nirmala were too normal to me that I didn't think about explaining those to her.

The first weekend we were going somewhere in our Volkswagen bug, a red one that I bought when I started to live off campus, and I stopped for a red light. I was looking at the light and hoped it would change because of my staring at it when Nirmala hit me hard on my shoulder.

"What?" I was shocked and angry. Wives do not hit their husbands.

Her eyes were wide with shock, she held my right arm so tightly that it hurt, and she pointed at a couple leaning on the telephone pole and deeply absorbed in necking and heavy petting.

Nirmala put her hand on her mouth. I looked at them and for a few seconds didn't understand why she was shocked.

"Just like *kutta* and *billi*!" She quickly scribbled on her palm—cats and dogs.

I remembered my reaction and my telling Dan about the two students busy with each other like cats and dogs. I laughed, which only made Nirmala more upset. As a good Indian man, I should have done something to stop this abomination. But I knew better.

"Stop staring at them. It's bad manners," I admonished her. She didn't stop and couldn't stop, but the light had changed and I put my whole weight on the gas pedal. I was irritated when I saw she was looking back with her head craned outside the window. The young couple, oblivious to the cultural lesson they were imparting, remained busy.

❖

We both knew, as Chuck had envisioned, she needed to learn English. I wanted her to learn to speak English. Babuji, my father, had her tutored in English. She knew the alphabet and a rudimentary vocabulary. However, she couldn't understand someone speaking English. I researched and found evening English as a second language (ESL) classes and registered her. Three times a week I would drive her to the class and then drive to Chuck and Margie's home in Georgetown where I drank beer and played chess. After two hours, I would pick her up. Her progress in class was slow but steady. However, she was learning more English outside of the classroom from talking to Surinder, Rajesh, and Ravi but mostly from television. She liked to hear news and sometimes switched on soap operas. Who said television was bad for learning?

Until she was able to understand English well, I had to "interpret" for her. In a store or when dealing with people who didn't know signs, I was forced to use my heavily accented Himachali English. If people didn't understand me, I would write. Slowly, Nirmala began to understand people and it became a team effort. I would speak and she would hear. This way, communication became possible, albeit slow and cumbersome.

Nirmala learned to speak and understand English and became fluent over time. However, she neglected to learn how to spell words properly. English is not a phonetic language and one needs to learn both spelling and phonology. Her problem was the exact opposite of mine. I pronounced words as they are written; she spelled the words as they are spoken. As she picked up signs and finger spelling and began to interpret for me in social settings and in stores, her finger spelling began to send me into a tizzy.

Her biggest problem was, and is, mixing up the "b" with the "v" sound. She also substitutes "g," "s," "j," and "z" sounds among these liberally and, for me, mercilessly. "F" and "ph" are, of course, a problem for everyone. Her adventures in freestyle spelling (that's what I call it) were fine if it was just one word and it was just us talking to each other. This became a major cause of possible cardiac arrests for me whenever she interpreted while dealing with salesmen, lawyers, doctors, and other professionals. For example, "go get me a drink from the w-a-r" requires some time to absorb. She liked to drink J-I-N-J-E-R ale (ginger ale), Kirk and Annette lived in V-A-S-T-A-N (Boston? Yes, let them guess) and G-A-N-F-A-R was Jennifer. The other problem was, and this became more serious with time, her habit of abbreviating words. Vacuum was too long to spell, so it became V-A-M. Other contractions were easier to follow. "Damn" shortened to "dam" made sense, but "calm" spelled as "kam" didn't. I had to depend on the context for such nuggets as L-A-T (turn off or on). The spelling torture was endless. My suggestions for her to try to pay attention to spelling while reading were ignored. Her reasoning was "you can spell good enough for both of us." Later, when our kids were born, her reasoning not to learn spelling was reinforced with "I got three excellent spellers here." The erratic adventure of her spelling increased with her vocabulary. I have become an expert at deciphering her phonetic spellings, but transposition of "b" with "v" and "g" with either "j" or "z" or "s" still confuses me to the point of going crazy. A "singer" could be a "zinger."

35

Settling Down in America

AFTER WAITING FOR SIX MONTHS TO HEAR FROM ANY school in India, I began to wonder if they really wanted me. In my ignorance, I had thought my master's degree in deaf education from the United States was a big deal. It wasn't. I had written in my cover letter that I was deaf. Deaf was a hot commodity as a teacher in the United States and still is. But it wasn't in India, and it still isn't.

Dr. Nomeland, who was the acting director of KDES at that time, told me that I had to have a work permit if I wanted to teach next year. To play it safe, I started the process and applied for a green card through KDES and received it in a few months. This would allow me to stay as long as I wanted or until I had a job in India.

Kirk suggested that I should make good use of my stay in America. I could use the resources here and my own experience to help various projects in India. My big dream was to have Indian Sign Language recognized as a language just like American Sign Language (ASL) was in the United States. Only, at that time no one called it ASL. It was still just sign language. Lou Fant's book used the term "Ameslan." There were a lot of various ideas about what sign language was. Bernard Bragg came up with the term "Ameslish"—American Sign English. He contended that since signs were used in English word order, it should have the word "English" in it.

When I learned ASL in the classroom and from my friends in 1967, one thing impressed me was that signs were used in English word order. A person could talk and sign at the same time. They called it Simultaneous Communication, or SimCom, at that time. I couldn't talk in Hindi or English and sign Indian Sign Language at the same. I thought that ASL was an "advanced" language and the Americans had "enriched" it. SimCom helped facilitate communication in a group composed of signers and nonsigners. I thought this was a good thing. However, I knew before anything else, I need to work on having a dictionary of Indian Sign Language.

As a first step toward this effort, I sent a letter and a survey form to the 117 schools for the deaf listed in a directory published by the All India Federation of the Deaf. Kirk helped me draft the letter and I got some help from KDES in getting those typed, copied, and addressed. Such a task in a world before personal computers was indeed daunting and very time consuming.

Of the 117 schools, only about thirty responded. But the responses were encouraging. Most didn't believe that there was Indian Sign Language. They did acknowledge that deaf people used some kind of mixture of gestures and signs to communicate among themselves. Having used ISL myself for six years, I knew there was an ISL but had to prove this by documenting its existence. The responding principals also offered to help with the research.

My knowledge about linguistics and research at that time was nil and I needed help. Gallaudet, being the Mecca of the Deaf world, had plenty of resources, more resources than in any other part of the world at that time. Dr. William Stokoe had established the Linguistics Research Laboratory (LRL) and had a few linguists working for him. I called and made an appointment with him to seek help. He told me to come over at lunch.

He was eating a sandwich and drinking a bottle of beer when I got to his office. He told me, pointing to his beer bottle, that he made that beer in his home. I was impressed. The guy had a few talents. How did he find time for making beer while being busy with research work?

After listening to me about my plans to develop a dictionary of ISL, he nodded approvingly. He said he was very busy and couldn't help at that time but would let me know when he could do something. I was glad that the great man was willing to help.

But the help didn't come. I waited for a few months and was wondering what to do when Mandira Banerjee, a hearing graduate student from India, suggested that I see Dr. James Woodward. She was in his class and had mentioned to him about my plans. Dr. Woodward—Mandira called him Woody—was interested.

I had heard of Woody but wasn't sure if he could really help. If Dr. Stokoe couldn't help, how could Woody? I asked myself. Still, I decided to see him, as there was no other recourse. Perhaps, I thought, he would help me get support from Dr. Stokoe.

Woody was more friendly and, more than that, helpful. He said he was very interested and would start trying to get funding for my project. I was elated. Woody was really interested in helping me. At the same time I wondered if he would follow up or forget my request.

Woody didn't forget. Within a month I got a note asking me to come over and see him. He had applied and received a small grant for travel and other expenses to do preliminary research on ISL in India. I wrote to Kirk and told him of the good news. It was decided that Woody, Kirk, and I would go to India in the summer for two weeks to collect preliminary data on ISL. There was no money for other expenses, so we had to pay for our own hotel and food as well as ground transportation. This was fine with us.

With Woody and Kirk's input, we decided to collect 120 signs from four major cities in India—Calcutta, Bombay, Delhi, and Madras—as each city had several schools for the deaf and an active Deaf community. I contacted the All India Federation of the Deaf (AIFD) for support. The general secretary then, D. K. Nandy, was very excited and helpful. The AIFD also donated one thousand rupees (about $50 at that time) for the project. This may sound low, but keeping in mind the limited resources the AIFD had, it was huge. We were thankful to them.

I contacted major schools in each city and had to eliminate Madras from our plans, as no one responded from there. We added Bangalore as a substitute, as it met all the criteria. We had hosts in each city: the AIFD in Delhi, the Oral School in Calcutta, Father Harry Stocks in Bangalore, and Father Freddy in Bombay.

The hosts in each city had entirely different backgrounds, which was encouraging. The AIFD, of course, being an organization of deaf people, was interested, and I had worked closely with them for six years. Kirk and I had met Father Harry in Bangalore at Gallaudet when he was visiting one summer. He had been living in Bangalore since 1966 and was doing a yeoman's service for deaf people there as well as spreading sign language. Father Freddy, who was a Jesuit priest, and I became friends when he attended Gallaudet for a semester in 1972. The Oral School in Calcutta was a mystery. The word "oral" and the gesture of offering to help research sign language was touching and inspiring.

I was scared as I made plans. Something might go wrong, I worried. Kirk kept bugging me about making sure there were no faux pas and his ongoing reminders didn't help my confidence. This was the first time that I was involved in such a project with international travel and the involvement of hundreds of people in each city.

The three of us arrived in Delhi in July. It was hot and humid. Eleven years in America had softened me and the heat bothered me. But Kirk and Woody seemed to take this all in a stride. They learned the British finger spelling and start to pick up ISL signs as they went. They could communicate with my deaf friends fairly well after a couple of days in Delhi.

In each city, we had three people provide us signs for the listed vocabulary. If all three or at least two gave the same sign, it was chosen for photographing. Woody transcribed all signs using Stokoe's transcription system. We also filmed some free conversation to analyze grammar.

In Delhi, I had arranged room for Kirk and Woody with a friend and I stayed with my brother Narain. In Bangalore, Harry Stocks took care of room and board through his mission. In Bombay and Calcutta, we stayed at cheap YMCA hotels. Mandira, who had moved back to India, helped in Bombay with transportation. Thus, we had help in each city in one form or another. This made us feel the work we were doing had a lot of support.

Woody and Kirk with a group of deaf volunteers who provided signs for the dictionaries.

Of course, we collected signs and later analyzed them. The results were published in the *Indian Journal of Applied Linguistics* and presented at the International Conferences on Applied Linguistics in Montreal, Canada. However, the greatest impact of this trip on deaf and hearing people in India was that two hearing people signed like deaf people. Kirk and Woody were both fluent in ASL. They signed all the time when I was around. At times, people thought they were deaf. Why hearing people would sign so well was a mystery to people in India, again, both deaf and hearing.

The attitude of some of the people I had contacted through my letters was interesting. I had not told them I was deaf. We would meet people and they would come smiling, shake hands, and start talking to me. When they learned I was deaf, they would look first surprised, then disappointed, and finally, a bit upset. Kirk and Woody were shocked at this attitude toward deafness. After learning that I was deaf, they would ignore me and focus on Woody and Kirk—two white hearing men.

Woody and Kirk would deflect their questions with "Madan is our leader. We are working for him." This didn't help much, but it was a good start. This attitude didn't bother me, but Kirk and Woody were irritated again and again.

Usually, the host would introduce us with "This is Dr. Woodward, this is Dr. Wilson, and this is—pause—a deaf boy from America." I didn't hear this introduction and kept smiling. But the expression on Woody's face would tell me something was wrong. Kirk thought it was funny even though he didn't feel comfortable with this attitude.

One evening while we were eating dinner, Woody had an idea.

"Why don't you get a PhD?" he asked matter-of-factly.

"What?" I was shocked at this suggestion. In 1977, there were perhaps ten deaf people who had a doctoral degree. I had never considered getting a doctoral degree. It was, to me, too lofty a goal. I also had a family to support. I was thirty-six. The term "nontraditional students" wasn't yet coined.

"Forget it, Woody," I said. "Let them call me deaf boy. Getting a PhD degree will not change their attitude. I am the first deaf person from India to get an MA degree and I am sure that most of these people calling me 'boy' do not have even a BA degree. They still think of themselves superior to me because of their hearing."

Woody and Kirk gave up. But little did they know they had sowed a seed in my mind that was going to germinate soon. A year later, I started taking classes part-time and the following year quit teaching at KDES and was a full-time PhD student at Gallaudet.

In the beginning I wanted to get the degree for the sake of getting it. Then the thought of putting a tail in front of my name, being back in the classroom to learn new skills, and the new career options that it might open began to shape up.

John Spellman, then my supervisor at KDES, wrote a strong recommendation letter for my admission to Gallaudet. Privately, he told me that I was chasing a wild goose. "Do not forget you are deaf. After you get a PhD degree, they perhaps will stop calling you 'deaf boy from America' and will start calling you 'Dr. Deaf Boy from America!'"

John Spellman is long gone, but he was right.

Graduating with my PhD. With me are my wife Nirmala, daughter Neerja, and son Dheeraj.

36

The Four Dictionaries

AFTER RETURNING FROM OUR DATA COLLECTION AND field research in India during the summer of 1977, life became pretty busy. Nirmala and I had one son, Dheeraj, and another baby on the way. I was taking two classes at Catholic University in the evenings and also analyzing the data we had collected. This was like having two jobs. Nirmala, who loves work, got busier. She took care of the house and Dheeraj and baby-sat a few kids. Due to her pregnancy, her energy level was very low, but the more she worked, the more energetic she became. This helped me focus on my job, classes, and research work.

I met Woody often and also took a linguistics class to develop some basic understanding of the field. However, I learned a lot about sign language linguistics by talking to him, Dennis Cokely, and Sue De Santis while hanging around the Linguistic Research Laboratory. They answered my questions and helped me learn more and more. They didn't ridicule my dream of "developing" ISL in the footsteps of ASL so that people could use ISL simultaneously while speaking Hindi, Marathi, and other languages. SimCom, however, was an abomination to linguists. It was like speaking Spanish and English at the same time, or like speaking Hindi using the word order of English language or vice versa. They humored me about my dream but did not encourage me. However, I got the message.

Woody managed to get another grant. This time, we were going to develop a comprehensive dictionary of Indian Sign Language. Kirk was busy finishing his doctorate at that time and had started his own research company. He didn't have the time to help us, so Woody enlisted support from Susan De Santis, his associate. They made a good team and I got along with them very well. While we were planning our expedition, Woody and Sue developed an affinity for Nirmala's cooking. We often met in our house in Laurel, where Woody and Sue ate dal with rice with great pleasure. They both had become vegetarians. Woody, who was also working on his black belt in karate, could eat enough dal to fill a horse. Sue's effort to have Woody eat less only made him more ravenous. Nirmala, of course, was happy about it. The best praise for one's cooking is watching your guests eat it as if there was no tomorrow.

Woody and Sue decided that since the initial research shows that there are four varieties of ISL in the four regions from where we collected sign samples, we should have four separate dictionaries to keep the integrity of each variety. I would have preferred one dictionary but had enough respect for their linguistic expertise to go with the idea. Then they decided that since it was my idea and I was doing all the planning, I should be the principal author of the dictionaries. That was a bit hard to swallow at first. People with the expertise should be the principal authors. However, they were adamant and getting glories is not exactly against my nature. So I agreed.

I started to contact all the good people who had helped us in 1977 for support with the big project now. The idea that there will be a dictionary of Indian Sign Language was a strong motivating factor for all of them. The All Indian Federation of the Deaf, which owned and operated two printing presses, agreed to publish the first dictionary. Things were moving.

We spent most of the summer of 1979 in India. Woody and Sue had another project, so they first went to Taiwan and joined me in Delhi. Nirmala and I flew with the kids—now two of them, as Neerja was born in 1978—directly to Delhi. Nirmala took the kids to Gagret, my ancestral home, and Lohara, her parents' home, while I traveled with Woody and Sue.

This time around, the task was huge. Instead of the 120 words, we had to collect all possible signs for the dictionary. We spent over a week in each city and worked all day. The monsoons had set in and the heat and humidity weren't helping. Somehow, Woody and Sue tolerated the weather better than I did, despite my having grown up in India.

In each city, we were amazed at the number of deaf people volunteering to provide signs. They came all dressed in their best clothes for the important occasion. Their language was being recognized and put in a book. This was a thing of great joy and pride for them and they helped with open hands and hearts.

The main problem was picking the right models. As in any country, late deafened or hard of hearing persons became leaders in the Deaf community. These leaders weren't always fluent signers, but they wanted to be known as the experts. Our criteria—born deaf, attended a school for the deaf, used ISL since childhood as the main mode of communication—excluded these leaders. They were born hearing, had attended public schools, spoke fluently, and used ISL only with deaf people. However, they were the leaders and it was hard for them to accept the fact that young deaf people who couldn't read and write were better suited for providing input on ISL. The same attitude prevailed in every city. We had to be very diplomatic in order to get them to allow the indigenous speaker of ISL to help us.

First, we three would sit with the selected volunteers and have them provide a sign for each word or concept. Woody and Sue would transcribe the most commonly used signs. Later, we would record these using two or three models. Sue and Woody would elicit the sign and I would take photographs. As we progressed, we began to work faster and faster. We became "experts" in collecting and documenting signs.

We had each film developed and printed right in the city to make sure the photographs were properly exposed and signs clear. We found a young deaf artist in Delhi who could draw the signs from photographs very clearly. His name was Vishnu. He had a full-time job but agreed to draw the signs from photographs for a nominal charge. He was more interested in the dictionary being published than making money. It was so nice to meet people like him.

We brought Vishnu's work and all the photographs back with us. I got busy with my studies and a part-time job. It took me more than a year to add information on the movement of hands and do the Hindi translation. Now the question was how to get it to the AIFD and find the money to print it. Since each dictionary required a lot of time, we decided to first focus on the dictionary on the Delhi variety of ISL. The other three dictionaries had to wait.

I contacted Dr. Robert Davila, then vice president of the Pre-College Programs—as the present Clerc Center was known then—and requested help. I was into my second year of the PhD program and was working full-time as his assistant. He told me he didn't have funds for international work but would try to find a way. A week later, he told me that I would get $2,000 to print the dictionary. Now all that was left was to save some money for the airfare to India. Nirmala and I cut corners and managed to save over $1,000 for my travel.

This was the first time I traveled to India as an American citizen. Nirmala and I had become citizens in 1979. At first, the thought of becoming American citizens never really crossed our minds since a green card allows a person all the benefits of a citizen except for voting. Most Americans don't exercise that right, anyway. However, my elder brother Narain expressed a desire to come to America for a few years as did Nirmala's young brother. The only way we could bring them here was to become American citizens.

It was not an easy decision in the beginning. I am sure it is not easy for any immigrant to change nationality. However, we had lived in America for more than a decade, our kids were American, and all our friends were also American. I was sure by then that I was not going back to India for a long time. So we both applied for becoming citizens and took the pledge very proudly along with more than fifty other people.

As an American citizen, I had to go to the Indian embassy to get a visa to visit India. That was a strange experience. I remembered how much work and time it took to get a student visa to the United States. Now I needed a visa to visit India.

In Delhi, I talked with Dilip Nandy, general secretary of the AIFD, and gave him $2,000 to print the dictionary. He told me to work with Mr. Bhat, then director of the Multipurpose Technical Training Center (MPTTCD) located in Hauz Khas in New Delhi. The MPTTCD had about forty deaf students who attended their photography, printing, sewing, and fitting training programs. Mr. Bhat focused all his energies on the printing press and the sewing department, which he ran like a business. He had sublet the press and the sewing departments to some business. Not much education or training was taking place in the photography and fitter departments. Of course, there were no students in the printing press and sewing departments. It was a sad state of affairs. The students and the staff were open with me and complained about the lack of training. They were afraid of Mr. Bhat as he would have thrown anyone who complained out of the school. I sat down with him once and tried to discuss the lack of education and training, but he ridiculed me. "They are fine," he said in a hurry and became busy with his paperwork.

I asked him if he could print the dictionary while I was there. He said that wasn't possible as the printing press had several deadlines to meet. He agreed that he would print it within the month and send me a few copies. He took the manuscript from me and placed it in a store room. "It will be safe here and I will make sure it is printed," he assured me again. I went back to Mr. Nandy, who shook his head. It was clear that he had little or no control over Mr. Bhat. However, he promised that he would push him to print the book soon. I returned to Gallaudet.

A month passed and then a second. No copies of the book arrived. I wrote to Mr. Bhat and Mr. Nandy. Mr. Bhat didn't respond. Mr. Nandy said he would have the book printed soon. Even after six months, there was no book.

It was obvious we couldn't depend on Mr. Bhat. There was something wrong. We also wondered what had happened to the $2,000 I had given to Mr. Nandy. It was obvious that writing letters wasn't going to get the book published. The fact that the original manuscript was somewhere in Mr. Bhat's office didn't help. Woody, Sue, and I got together and decided to go to India. I applied for and got a travel grant from the National Science Foundation. Woody and Sue got some support from Gallaudet and used some from their own resources. Early in January, the three of us flew to Delhi.

First we visited the offices of the All India Federation of the Deaf. Mr. Nandy and his staff were very cordial and helpful but didn't know what was going on with the dictionary. Mr. Nandy said that he had asked Mr. Bhat repeatedly and that Mr. Bhat had told him that the book was almost ready. He suggested that we go see Mr. Bhat. It was obvious again that despite being Mr. Bhat's boss, Mr. Nandy had no control over him.

We drove to Hauz Khas and were warmly greeted by Mr. Bhat. He had tea brought in and while we sipped tea and made small talk, he kept receiving other visitors or going out for a few minutes in the middle of our conversation. Mr. Bhat had become deaf at the age of twenty or so. He spoke like a hearing person and lipread some or pretended to. What irked me was that he would talk without signing.

Woody kept asking where the printed book was and Bhat kept saying he would show us soon. We got tired and finally Woody blew up, yelled at Bhat and wrote to him, "How long will you keep stalling? Madan left the manuscript six months ago. Where are the printed copies?"

This didn't faze Bhat. He called his peon and said something to him in Hindi. The peon left and came back after a few minutes and told something to Bhat. Bhat yelled at the peon and then told us that he couldn't find the book. We got really worried. Bhat was pulling something, though we didn't understand what.

We all were angry, but Bhat kept smiling as if we didn't matter. He was the boss there and wanted to save face. He tried to look busy by shuffling piles of paper as if we weren't there. We three walked out and went to the photography section. My old friend Vasant with whom I had worked at a photography shop in the 1960s was a teacher there. He told us that Bhat had done nothing as he was busy making money printing "orders from hearing people." He then led us to the basement and opened the door of the storeroom where I had last seen Bhat put the manuscript. To my relief and also horror, the manuscript was still sitting exactly the same place. There were sole marks on it. Someone had stood on it while trying to reach something on a high shelf. We picked the manuscript up. It was dusty and dirty from six months of sitting in a store room. We left without saying good-bye to Bhat.

We told the whole story to Nandy and expressed our outrage. Nandy made the same excuses of Bhat being Bhat and promised that he will take care of everything and print the book in the other press that the AIFD owned and operated.

I left the next day as my two-week leave was over. Woody and Sue stayed and worked closely with Nandy and his assistants to make sure that work on printing had started. Nandy had assigned Onkar Sharma, who had worked with AIFD since its inception in 1955 and was a good friend of mine, to supervise the project. Nandy and Sharma were true to their word and the book, *An Introduction to Indian Sign Language: Focus on Delhi*, was published in 1982.

With the Delhi variety taken care of, we needed to find money and publishers for the other three books. Fr. Harry Stocks had promised to print the Bangalore dictionary. However, my letters to him didn't produce any answer. That was unlike Harry and made me wonder what was going on.

In the summer of 1985, my niece, Narain's daughter Vaneeta, was getting married. Weddings provide the perfect time for meeting with all the family. Each time I went to India with my wife and children, I left a few family members upset. Traveling all the way from America and

then visiting all family members spread out in different cities and villages was very difficult and time consuming. A marriage brings the whole
family together. So I decided to take my family for a month to India.
We could attend the wedding, meet all the relatives, have Dheeraj and
Neerja—then ten and seven years old—exposed to their roots, and have
the dictionaries published.

After the wedding, I went to visit Prag. Prag is my eldest sister's eldest
son. I am his uncle, but being only four years older than him, we grew
up as friends rather than uncle and nephew. Each winter and summer
when schools were closed, Prag would come to Gagret and stay there for
months. We shared books, saw movies together, and talked about things
like two preteenage and later teenage friends do. As we grew up, however, we saw little of each other. He went to medical school and I went
to America. We continued to exchange letters for most of our lives. Prag
drove us to Mukatsar, a small town in western Punjab, not far from the
Pakistani border. I need to diverge here as I had had the opportunity to
see Prag in action. This will give one a good idea of how surgeries were
performed in India. He asked me if I wanted to join him and being always
curious, I agreed.

Before entering the operating theater, Prag pointed to the sign on the
door and we both took our shoes off. After a short hallway, there was
an anteroom where a couple of stretchers and odds and ends were lying.
Prag put on flip-flops and went into the surgery room.

A man lay there on a table with an IV in his arm and both feet sticking
out from a blanket. Two men were working on his toes. Both toes had
huge gashes with blood still flowing. One guy was stitching the big right
toe and the other guy was putting some medication on the left toes. A
woman was sitting on the floor soaking plaster-coated gauze bandages.
At that time, a young boy about fifteen came in and, apparently at Prag's
order, gave me his flip-flops. I put those on as the floor was ice cold.

The patient didn't wince in pain so I assumed he was under local
anesthesia. I asked Prag and he confirmed my observation. He told me
that the patient had multiple fractures in his lower right leg and only
lacerations in most of the toes. While he was writing these details on his
palm with his index finger and gesticulating, the two guys working on the
toes and the woman who was sitting on the floor soaking plaster-coated
gauze bandages become more interested in this communication than their

respective chores. Prag apparently introduced me to them and went into a detailed spiel about me. The stitching and cleaning of the wounds as well as the rinsing of gauze bandages stopped while the four people took in whatever hyperbole Prag was feeding them. I looked at the patient, who had opened his eyes and was looking at me with more interest than in his own predicament. Prag showed me the X-ray slides. They were clear. Even I could tell where the bones were broken. He was going to set them up and then put the cast on.

He showed me an X-ray machine that showed slides live on two CRT screens. He explained on his palm how only 10 percent of orthopedic surgeons in India had those machines. The rest set bones by guesswork, just like he had done until a few years earlier when he had purchased this very expensive machine.

The stitching over, the two guys helped Prag move the surgery table in order to use the X-ray machine. Prag and the two assistants put on heavy protective gear, the kind dentists throw on you when they X-ray your teeth. Soon, I could see the broken bones below the knee and in the heel area pictured on the two screens. Prag moved the patient's foot and lower leg around until he was satisfied with the setting of the bones. Two of his assistants helped him while he rolled cotton bandages around the patient's leg. After that, very slowly, he rolled the soaked gauze bandages sprinkled heavily with plaster of Paris over the cotton bandage. He checked the bone setting several times and repeated the process of rolling plaster of Paris three more times.

The process over, the patient was rolled onto a stretcher and wheeled out of the surgery room. Prag told me that another patient was waiting. I asked him if it was OK to bring Nirmala in as she might want to watch the process. He was happy to have her join us, so I ran out, put on my shoes, and went to the residence side of the hospital. Nirmala was interested and Rita, Prag's wife, decided to join us. We three marched back to the operation theater, where the lady lady who soaked the bandages in plaster of Paris was eating *jalebis*—a popular Indian candy. I couldn't believe how someone could eat right after this bloody surgery. However, for them it was just routine, like my typing this story.

Nirmala, after taking in the scenery and seeing some blood splattered on the floor, changed her mind and raced outside of the surgery room. I had to follow her out.

❖

After spending a few days in Gagret, we returned to Delhi and then I decided to travel to Bangalore and Bombay. The main goal was to find Fr. Harry and have him publish the Bangalore dictionary. At the same time, I wanted the family to travel to other Indian cities. I had little money left, so we traveled by train.

After two days' journey, we arrived tired and disheveled. I sent a letter to Fr. Harry informing of my coming with the manuscript and asking him if he could meet us at the railway station and also to provide us with room while we were there. At the railway station platform, I couldn't see one white face and wondered what to do, when a friendly man came to us, shook hands, and hugged me. I felt relieved. This was Joe, Fr. Harry's assistant. Harry, said Joe, was in Canada for the summer for his annual vacation. I knew "vacation" meant that Harry was back home collecting funds for various projects.

Joe took us to the huge four-story building where they had a large vocational training program for the deaf. This was Harry's dream, the result of his decades of hard work. After setting us in a guestroom, Joe gave us a tour of the facilities. They trained young deaf people in fitter work, printing, and carpentry, among other things. I was more interested in the press and his willingness to print the dictionary. He told me that it wouldn't be a problem and that he would do it.

"Just leave the manuscript with me and I will have it printed," he assured me. This bothered me a bit. In the past, he always deferred to Fr. Harry. Now, he was talking as if he was in charge of everything. Maybe, I thought, Harry believed in delegation and had been grooming Joe to take over after he retired. Later, after I returned to America, I learned Joe had indeed taken over, but on his own. He wanted to get out of Harry's shadow and using his connection in the immigration department, forced Harry to leave India. Thus, Joe had pulled a *coup d'état* against Harry and taken over a fledging organization, only to use it for his personal gains. A few years later, deaf people threw Joe out and took over. The Bangalore dictionary got lost in this struggle for power. There were no takers for Calcutta and Bombay dictionaries. In the end, Woody decided to publish them as monographs through the Gallaudet Research Institute. I learned that doing work in India while living in the United States wasn't easy and it didn't bear as much fruit as one wanted.

37
Moving On

WHILE WORKING ON MY DISSERTATION, I STARTED TO apply for administrative jobs all over America. I thought with my experience and degrees, I would be offered a principal's job in a school for the deaf in no time. I was living in a fantasy world just like when I had applied for teaching positions in India ten years earlier.

There wasn't even one response to my applications. I had applied for all levels—supervisor, principal, assistant superintendent, superintendent—but no one asked me to come over for an interview. I was puzzled, but Dr. Delgado, who was still the dean of Gallaudet's graduate school, and Dr. Edmund Skinski, chairman of the department from where I was getting my degree, weren't. Skinski called me to his office and jokingly told me I should change my name.

"What is wrong with my name?" I asked. He was a funny guy and I really liked him. He didn't seem to be joking.

Ed Skinski told me that he was following my efforts to get a job and had talked to two superintendents who had contacted him for possible candidates. Ed had proposed my name and never did get any positive feedback. One of them finally did confide in him. "Look, Ed, you want me to hire someone whose name I can't even spell or pronounce?"

This was 1982. All superintendents for the schools were white men. There were one or two deaf superintendents. Here I was, an Indian deaf man asking for the top job. It was obvious my degree didn't help. There were some superintendents who had only an MA degree. But they weren't deaf or people of color.

I had never thought of ever being discriminated against in America. At Gallaudet, I had forgotten that I was from India and looked different from other students. Neither teachers nor students had ever let me feel that way. Now, suddenly someone who meant well was asking me

157

to change my name to something like John Smith or Richard Jones. Of course, Ed was joking, but his joke spoke volumes about the problem.

Dr. Delgado had another idea. He knew several superintendents and decided to contact them, asking them to give me an internship at a nominal salary. He thought that once I got one foot in and impressed them, I could get a permanent job there. He wrote letters to six superintendents he knew well. He told them about me and how it would greatly benefit me working with them for a semester. Two of them showed some interest, but later said they didn't have any money to pay or a place to stay. So Delgado's plans to get my one foot in some place didn't work.

During my final year in the program when I was working on my dissertation, I started working full-time as an assistant for long-range planning in Dr. Schuchman's office. He was the provost then and knew me since I was his student. I worked with Dr. David McGuinness, a mathematics professor who was on loan to the provost's office. Working with Dave was a great experience for me. He was very creative and imaginative. I learned a lot about planning, much more than I had learned in the classroom. I liked the job and thought if nobody wanted me out there in schools for the deaf, I was going to stay here. The salary was good and the opportunity of working with top administrators was fulfilling. I learned which deans were so good and hard-working and also which deans didn't know what they were doing and didn't care. How they had risen to their respective positions was a mystery to me.

The Deaf world is a small world. Everyone knows everyone else. This smallness helps people and also hurts them. I got my first taste of this smallness when I applied to the Texas School for the Deaf (TSD). The superintendent of TSD was Dr. Victor Galloway. I had met Vic many times when he worked at Model Secondary School for the Deaf (MSSD); however, we were only on greeting terms. I saw the advertisement for the supervisor of the middle school at TSD. I thought that supervisor was not a high enough level for a person holding a PhD degree. But Ed encouraged me to apply for it telling me that TSD was a large school and Vic knew me and, perhaps, wouldn't be scared by the fact that my name was hard to spell.

I sent the application and forgot about it. Vic knows me, but other people in Texas do not. They will have a problem with spelling my name. However, I was surprised to get an invitation from TSD for an interview.

I wasn't sure if I was going to get that job or even I wanted it, but it would be a good experience being interviewed, so I accepted.

A teacher from the middle school came to pick me up from the motel I was staying. She was very abrupt and didn't look friendly at all. Obviously, she wasn't very thrilled about my bid to become her boss. It was just fine with me. As we entered the campus of TSD, I had a cultural shock. I was used to working and living at Gallaudet. The TSD campus in late October looked shabby. There were no lawns and the buildings were unkempt. It was depressing, and I felt like telling the teacher to take me back to the motel. But they had paid for my round-trip airfare and I owed them at least the pleasure of an interview.

Since I had lost interest in the job, I answered questions recklessly. I wasn't nervous, and I gave answers without thinking and pontificated in the hope that they would be turned off and not offer me the job. An old classmate who taught there showed me around the campus. At Gallaudet he had been a big football jock, and we didn't hang around together during our college years. He was friendly but not very encouraging. I was happy when all of this was over and flew back to Washington that night. I told Nirmala I didn't want that job. She was relieved. Much as she did want me to get a better administrative job, she didn't want to move from Maryland and from her house. Nirmala wasn't much on change.

To my surprise, Vic called the next day on a TTY, the Teletype phone. I thought he had some additional questions, but to my surprise, he offered me the job. The salary was slightly less than what I was making at Gallaudet and I used this as an excuse.

"Dr. Galloway," I told him, "I cannot afford to lose money and move all the way to Texas."

"Do you know Texas has no state tax? And the difference between your present salary and what we are offering will be more than made up," said Vic, the good salesman.

We went back and forth and finally, Vic gave up. I wondered if I had made the right decision and was still wondering when Dr. William Marshall, one of my professors in the administration department, called and asked me to come see him.

I walked over to Fowler Hall and met with Bill. He took me to a classroom from his office, made me sit in a chair, and stood next to the blackboard.

"What are your long-term goals?" he asked. We had discussed that in our classes before.

"To be a superintendent of a school for the deaf," I replied.

Bill wrote "superintendent" and drew a circle around it.

"What do you need to plan for this goal?" The professor was acting more like a lawyer.

I thought about it and told him how I would work as a principal and then as an assistant superintendent and so forth.

Bill wrote the position names and drew arrows from them to the circled "superintendent" and then put the chalk down. His writing was done.

"So," he asked me clapping his hands to get rid of chalk dust, "you plan to become a superintendent of a school for the deaf by working as an assistant in the provost's office?"

I had no answer to that. While I was thinking, he added, "You get out of Gallaudet and fast if you want to move up."

I walked out dazed and thought about what Bill had said. Back in my office, after thinking more for about five minutes, I called Vic and told him that I was coming to Austin and asked what date would be good.

Then I called Nirmala, who got upset at this decision. Why? She kept asking on the TDD. I told her to wait and we would talk more at home. It took a long time to convince her that it was a good move. Leaving the house where we had lived for seven years and where our children were born and had grown up was unthinkable to her. I wasn't going back on my promise and was adamant.

I was never sorry about this decision. It opened new challenges and the rise in my career was fast. After a year in Texas, I was promoted to associate principal and the six years in that position sharpened my skills. I moved to Illinois as an assistant superintendent and a year later, I was superintendent of Eastern North Carolina School for the Deaf. I had achieved my goal eight years after leaving Gallaudet.

38

The Career Ladder

SOME PEOPLE LIKE TO STAY IN ONE PLACE AND ARE SATIS-fied with their jobs and lives. Both the Bhagavad-Gita and the Bible suggest this. Be happy and satisfied with what you have. Do not hanker for more. I have not met anyone who follows this advice, especially in America where "keeping up with the Joneses" is the norm. I did follow the "not hankering for more" dictum, but only for a few seconds after reading the Bhagavad-Gita. Then the desire to join the rat race took over. If I were the "satisfied" type, I would still be herding cattle and be happy with my lot. Seeking "unhappiness," it seems, was in my blood.

While working as supervisor and later as associate principal of the East Campus of TSD, I kept applying for superintendent and assistant superintendent positions. I really enjoyed my job at TSD and had a lot of support from people both above and below me. However, the itch to move up and give up "satisfaction" and "happiness" pushed me to keep applying. Nirmala had finally accepted Texas as her home and was happy that she had moved here. She liked Austin and the friendly Texans. She also liked working part-time at TSD as a dormitory counselor. She was finally feeling at home and was wary of my restlessness. She kept telling me moving to another and higher job will only make me wish for still another higher job. "Where will it all end?" she asked. She was just paraphrasing the Bhagavad-Gita all over. Mostly she hated to pack and move to another place. A house to me was a house; for her it was a home.

Interestingly enough, the same cold shoulder I got for my applications while I was at Gallaudet surfaced again. I didn't get any response to my various applications. I thought at least they should interview me. My supervisor, Claire Bugen, said it could be a racial thing. "You are an Indian. How many Indians are working as administrators? How many Chinese?" She had a point, but somehow, I didn't take it. I felt America,

Wearing a Stetson hat at the Texas School for the Deaf with Claire Bugen
(principal) and Tarry Damarow (elementary supervisor).

being the land of opportunity, would not deny me just because my name
sounded funny. So I kept applying. It may sound like I was sending out an
application a week. Actually, it was perhaps two or three a year. Administration of schools for the deaf is a small niche.

Finally I got some interview calls. They came because someone at
those schools knew me personally or through another person. Claire
said, "The adage 'It is not what you know but who you know' works
very well in deaf education. People are at times hired before the positions
are even advertised." Come to think of it, my appointment as associate
principal of East Campus was assured to me by Vic Galloway, the superintendent, before it was advertised.

During that time, Vic Galloway had left TSD and moved on to California. After one year of uncertainty under two acting superintendents, the
TSD board hired Marvin Sallop from the Louisiana School for the Deaf.
Marvin came in with a lot of ideas and zeal. He encouraged me to apply for
jobs at other schools and offered to write glowing letters of recommenda-

tion. I wasn't sure if he really was interested in my career or just wanted me to move on. It seemed more of the latter, so I intensified my efforts.

I would have ended up staying at the Texas School for the Deaf if it wasn't for a historical development at Gallaudet that opened new doors for deaf people.

39

Advice—Good and Bad

WE ALL NEED ADVICE AND LOVE TO GIVE IT, ESPECIALLY unasked. I had my share of getting advice—both sought and forced on me—both good and bad advice. Bill Marshall's advice to get out of Gallaudet was some of the best I received. There are others that I still cherish.

Moving to Texas as a first-line supervisor, also known as a firing-line supervisor, was scary. As a teacher and administrative assistant, I had fun criticizing all the administrators and never ceased to wonder how dumb they were. Now, I was going to open myself to criticism by smart aleck people of my own ilk. This was not a very friendly situation.

So I began to seek advice from administrators I knew. Dr. Hicks, who was vice president of research at Gallaudet and who had been my dissertation advisor, gave me a real nugget.

"One big mistake people from Gallaudet do is tell people 'how we do it at Gallaudet.' You must forget Gallaudet and show respect for the local yokels. Texans have their own attitude. They don't need Gallaudet attitude there." I decided to follow it.

Bob Davila gave more practical advice. "First let people working for you know you as a person and then start showing your professional skills." He added, "by the way, I would lose this name-sign."

My name-sign at Gallaudet was, and still is, upside-down-thumb pressed on one's forehead and going up slightly, which is the sign for India or the Indian. "You are going to Texas, a Southern state. You do not need a racial or ethnic sign. Pick a new sign."

I followed this advice and am thankful for it. There was some advice that I didn't follow. One supervisor at KDES told me to "arrive early at work and greet teachers as they arrive and tell the latecomers, 'nice of you to finally decide to show up.'" I used my own device to work with latecomers.

A year later, when I had become friendly with my staff in the TSD middle school, one teacher told me that what they liked about me was that I wasn't the "big head from Gallaudet." Dr. Hicks had been right. That was a boom time in Austin and people from the East were flocking there for jobs and business opportunities. One common bumper sticker declared, "WE DO NOT GIVE A DAMN HOW YOU DO IT IN NEW YORK."

The students at TSD gave me a new name-sign—V on the right side of the chest. I carried this sign from Texas to other states. When I returned to Gallaudet, I was back to "the Indian" sign. Even Bob Davila uses it. Advice, after all, is to be given, not necessarily to be followed.

Years later, when I tried to thank Bob Davila for his advice about "letting people know you as a person first" he said pieces of advice come a dime a dozen. They become valuable only if and when one uses them. True enough.

40

Weeds Theory

LIKE EVERYONE ELSE, I LEARNED MOST OF MY LESSONS outside the classroom. We all face real-life experiences that have profound effects on us. I had my share of "learning on the street" and one of these experiences was in Austin, Texas.

We had moved to Austin in 1984. We bought a house in a community called Travis County. It was a nice community and a nice house. But I had a concern. The Great American Hobby of keeping lawns perfect had become a major problem for me. The neighbors on both sides had nothing else to do but to make sure their lawns looked perfect. They watered them regularly, mowed them each Saturday, and edged the lawn to make it look perfect. I told Nirmala that our neighbors paid more attention to their lawns than to their wives. She was curious: "How do you know?" Well, my observation wasn't very scientific.

Nirmala, who liked flowers and plants and had the house full with them and paid as much attention, if not more, than my neighbors did to their lawns, was concerned about our lawn. I did water it and I did mow it and I also edged it, but it didn't look half as beautiful as my neighbors' lawns. I thought it was my bad luck to have bought a house between two lawn-obsessed guys. However, walking around Travis County proved that almost all houses had lawns like my neighbors. I was glad to see one lawn that looked worse than mine. I wanted to shake hands with the owner, but then I saw a sign that the house was for sale. The lawn had been neglected for some time.

One Saturday morning when I was thinking about reading a couple of books, Nirmala, who, like all good wives, has the uncanny ability to read her husband's mind, pointed at me accusingly.

"Did you see our lawn?" I got worried. The question had the unmistakable bearing of some work for me.

"I see it all the time," I assured her. "It is beautiful!"

"It is full of weeds," she countered.

I wasn't aware of weeds. The lawn was green and there were some yellow flowers, which I thought gave a nice touch. The mixture of various kinds of "grass" in the lawn, in my opinion, made it more beautiful. Not to Nirmala, who admired the monotonous density of green grass on both sides of our house.

I felt depressed. There would be no book reading, I knew. I asked her what she wanted me to do. She already had done her research and had some discussions with the neighbors' wives. They had educated her how to totally destroy her husband's Saturday. I looked at Dheeraj and Neerja for support. They became very engrossed in the books they were reading. It was a clear message: I was on my own.

Nirmala produced a small tool, which looked like a long screwdriver but was a weed eradicator or antireading implement. She explained that I had to go out and get the weeds out. My efforts to postpone this event by a week was countered with her, "OK, I guess I have to do it myself." This is the worst kind of blackmail and I found myself squatting in the lawn in the hot Texans sun trying to weed. There were about a few million and I guessed I would be retired from my job at the Texas School for the Deaf by the time I was finished.

However, there is a God! A few minutes into my grunt work, I felt someone standing next to me. I wiped sweat off my eyes and looked. It was Bob, the neighbor on the right side. He was a nice guy even though he had a great lawn. He was smiling and I tried to figure out how much sarcasm was there, but the sun was in my eyes. Bob asked me to stop and come with him. I was very happy to stop and followed him to his house.

He showed me an advertisement for lawn fertilizer and told me to go buy three bags. I was puzzled.

"Look," I said, "I got those weeds to take care of. I will think about the fertilizer when I am done with them." In about twenty years, I thought to myself.

He shook his head and then using some writing and some gestures he assured me that if I fertilized the lawn, I wouldn't have to pull weeds. That was the magic word. I threw the weed-puller in the lawn and went inside my house and began to change clothes.

Nirmala was exasperated. She knew I hated physical work and must have found a way out of it.

"Now what?" she demanded.

I pointed the sales brochure to her and explained that I was going to buy some fertilizer.

"And what about the weeds?" Her hands were firmly placed on her hips.

I explained that it was Bob's secret to having a weedless lawn. I told her how this was Bob's idea. She calmed down, as she had a great respect for Bob's lawn and, therefore, for Bob and his ideas.

Together we went to a store called 84 and bought three bags of the fertilizer Bob had recommended. Bob loaned me his fertilizer spreader and I went around and around the lawn for over an hour spreading the multi-colored little granulates that looked like homeopathic pills. Spreading the fertilizer was a lot easier than pulling the weeds, so I was very happy.

After I was done, I watered the lawn and then went back to my book. Nirmala did try to find other work for me, but I was adamant and the book won.

We waited patiently. Each day, I checked the lawn and became an expert on weeds. What used to look like a lawn of grass now had many different kinds of weeds as well as some grass. Slowly, the weeds began to recede and more and more grass was visible. At the end of the month, I was surprised to see a major change in our lawn. It didn't look much worse than my neighbors', and the weeds were almost all gone.

I began to think of this miracle more because it saved me some hard grunt work than because of what it did for our lawn. I thought instead of focusing on the weeds and trying to get rid of them, I needed to focus on the grass and making it better by fertilizing it. I showed my respect for the grass and fed it with fertilizer and as its roots grew deeper and stronger, the weeds had no room to grow.

Translated into real life, I thought about how we should focus on good people working with us instead of wasting our time and energy on laggards. If one focused on good people, praised their work, rewarded them, the number of not-so-good people would go down. I promised myself that I would follow this practice as an administrator in school.

Still, weeds manage to survive. Who knows, maybe I am one of the weeds.

41

Deaf President Now!

AN IMPORTANT HISTORICAL EVENT IN DEAF EDUCATION happened in 1988, which changed the lives of Deaf people in America as well as around the world. It also indirectly affected careers of many Deaf people, including myself.

I was attending an international conference on bilingual education in Chicago, in March 1988. This conference had nothing to do with deafness, except that Margaret Walworth, who was still teaching at Gallaudet and had been involved in teaching English as a second language (ESL), was heavily involved in it. She had received permission from the organizers to have a seminar on deafness and had invited me to facilitate it. About fifteen Deaf people, mostly from Illinois and Indiana, were in attendance.

We all were wondering who the new president of Gallaudet would be. Some of the participants, including my old friend Margie Walworth and Jamie Tucker, had come from Gallaudet and filled us in on what was going on. This was the first time that three Deaf persons had applied for the position. Each of us had our "own candidate" and we were also worried that none of the Deaf candidates was going to be selected, which proved to be correct. Gallaudet's board of trustees selected a woman—Elizabeth Zinser—who had no background in deafness or deaf education. We were upset and were wondering what to do when the three networks and CNN broke the news that students at Gallaudet had started a protest and had barricaded the campus with chains and buses parked at the entrance. We watched the television in disbelief. It was the first time that deafness-related news was national news. There was Peter Jennings talking about the deaf students protest and about Gallaudet University. Then there was Ted Koppel on *Nightline* interviewing Marilee Matlin, the Oscar-winning movie star and Greg Hlibok, the student leader. Gallaudet had become mainstream news. The timing for this event was perfect. There was no war or flood dominating the news. Gallaudet got top billing thanks to the slow news period in the media.

What happened later is history. I. King Jordan became the first Deaf president of Gallaudet University. That might have been the most tangible result of this protest by the students; however, the impact was felt all over the world. When I had arrived in America in 1967, Gallaudet College was over one hundred years old, but only three miles from it, a cab driver and another person didn't know where Gallaudet College was. They had never heard of it.

After the protest, Gallaudet became a household name. You mentioned Gallaudet and people knew where it was and what it stood for. It became famous like Harvard and other universities. The national coverage for a full week had put Gallaudet on the map.

The biggest impact was on the Deaf people. For the first time, perhaps since the charter to establish Gallaudet was signed by President Lincoln, Deaf people and their rights were recognized. Lincoln may have started the college; it was the protest that brought Gallaudet to its full recognition. When I visited India, even hearing people there began to ask me about I. King Jordan and Gallaudet. Of course, here in America, Jordan was better known than the presidents of other universities.

Like many other Deaf professionals in education, I also began to get attention. It was just like in the 1970s. At that time demand for deaf teachers became very high. The demand for deaf administrators rose after the protest. I began to get responses to my applications and even personal calls asking me if I was interested in this or that position. King Jordan's catapult into Gallaudet's presidency had changed my status from "persona non grata" to, for lack of a Latin expression, a "persona wanted badly." The Gallaudet protest nullified my need to change my name also. Globalization of names had begun. During the next five years, I moved from the position of associate principal to assistant superintendent to superintendent of two different schools. In my interviews, I always declared to the selection committee, "I would like to be considered for this position not because of my deafness, but despite my deafness." Times had changed, and now I could make statements like that.

42

The National Conference on Education of the Deaf in a Time Warp

AT THE TIME WHEN STUDENTS AND FACULTY AT GALLAU-
det University were demanding a president who embodied deafness in
its pure form, I had an experience attending the National Conference on
Education of the Deaf (NCED) in India in January 2006. That sent me
back half a century or more. I had been living in the United States too
long to realize that things were very different in India.

I learned that the annual NCED was scheduled in January in Chennai.
I thought this was a great opportunity for me to meet Indian educators. I
contacted all my friends to get me invited to speak and they began to contact their various friends. I was told by my friends that they were assured
by their friends' friends that I would be welcomed as a speaker. After all,
how many deaf people in India have doctoral degree and how many had
held high positions like I did? Little did I know I was embarking on a
thorny path. It was a strange journey and helped me learn a few things
about people who ruled this organization and, therefore, deaf education
in India. I will use American names to ensure anonymity.

My friends, after waiting for news from their friends, advised me to
contact the organizers directly as they were not getting any response.
So I contacted Mrs. Alice and expressed my desire to participate in the
conference. She referred me to Dr. Bender who was the local program
chairman. My friends also got some contacts who referred me to Dr.
Bender, suggesting that I be invited.

The president of NCED, whom I knew personally, had informally
invited me to attend the conference in the past. However, due to
scheduling conflicts, I couldn't attend. I e-mailed her and she referred
me to the local host, whom I had already contacted. For two weeks

there was a hectic exchange of about fifty e-mails, but no invitation materialized. I contacted my contacts again and learned they were also getting a silent treatment. This intensified their efforts and my résumé was sent to the organizers and whoever was connected to the exalted organization.

I still received no invitation. This only made me more eager and I went ahead and made plane reservations from Washington, DC, to Delhi to Chennai so I could be there January 23–25. I was sure that if I showed up, they might allow me to speak for even ten minutes. Unbridled optimism is a wonderful asset but also can get you deep in something.

Then I got an e-mail from Mrs. Sarah, the director of a very successful oral school who was the local host. She said that Sister (Dr.) Rita Mary had informed her that only certified educators of the deaf can be allowed to attend the conference and that I should get further clarification from Sister Rita Mary. She is the godmother of deaf education and has been involved for about sixty years. She is a staunch supporter (and implementer) of oral education. I wrote to her immediately explaining that I had a master's degree in deaf education and taught deaf people from preschool to the doctoral level. I also wrote that in addition to having a teaching license in several states, I had taught in three teacher training programs. These credentials, I concluded in my e-mail to her, should "qualify me to attend the conference." There was no response from the Sister. Silence is golden, I guess.

I flew to Chennai and spent two nice days meeting my friend Jayshree and her family and staff of the Ability Foundation she directs. It was a great, positive experience. They are doing a great job by publishing a top-notch magazine and providing rehabilitation, training, and employment to the disabled. This prepared me for the humbling experience at the conference. Jayshree had her driver take me to the college where the conference was held. I was excited and also had some trepidation about my reception at this meeting of staunch oralists.

The driver, a good one, drove me all the way to the registration area outside the auditorium. He jumped out and opened the door for me. This got everyone's attention. A lady, who happened to be the local host, very nicely guided me to a chair in the front row. I looked at the 450-plus audience in the back hoping to see a friendly face. There were none. Then I saw Sister Rita Mary sitting nearby. I walked to her and said a nice hello. She jumped from her chair and offered it to me and walked away.

Her expression clearly showed that the chair she had offered me was the last place on earth she wanted me to be.

The meeting began. Invited dignitaries walked slowly on to the stage. I knew all of them and they knew me. It was a very interesting experience. I sat there smiling stupidly and looking at them. They were very aware of my being there. Some of them smiled at me when our eyes met and other looked away quickly. I felt good. Making people nervous gives you a warm feeling, even when you are being insulted.

There was an hour-long ceremony with garlands, lighting of lamps, and some short speeches. I kept looking at the important people sitting on the stage. No one was deaf. There were no interpreters. I looked back at the audience again. Obviously, there was not even one deaf person there. I had forgotten that there is not even one deaf teacher of deaf children in India.

All through the opening ceremonies, I divided my time looking at the faces of the people on whom the education of three million deaf children depended and thumbing notes on my Sidekick. After the ceremony, they all walked down and there was a ten-minute tea break.

Dr. Surinder Randhawa, whom I had met at Gallaudet while she was on a Fulbright scholarship and had become good friends with, had been helping me get invitation to speak at this conference. She arrived at that time and introduced me to Dr. Bender and asked that I be allowed to speak for ten minutes. Dr. Bender said that would be fine and that she would call me at 12:30 when the morning session would end. She also introduced me to Phalguni, a young teacher at a school for cochlear implanted children. She knew ISL well and said she would try to interpret for me. I felt more comfortable.

There were six twenty-minute sessions. I could follow these sessions easily as all had detailed PowerPoint slides and the presenters just read them. However, to show my appreciation, I kept looking at the volunteer interpreter.

None of the twenty-minute presenters spoke for twenty minutes. They rambled on in English. Surinder signed to me that most of the audience had little or no knowledge of English. Only the elite teachers knew English. Others, I assumed, understood less than me despite their being able to hear. I could read the slides on the screen. I felt better.

They stopped for lunch at 1:30—one hour late. Dr. Bender told me she would call me first thing after lunch. I joined Surinder and some other professionals for the lunch and met some people I knew before. I was amazed at the number of people who could sign but wouldn't. It was obvious they were not comfortable using signs in front of their peers. I talked to them and learned that the entrenched and dogmatic people with a lot of clout who were more interested in pushing their agenda than the welfare of deaf children were managing deaf education there. Their talks made me feel great. A good teacher knows communication is the key to teaching deaf children and would find ways to communicate.

After lunch, everyone returned to the auditorium. Dr. Bender kept her promise and handed me a cordless microphone and pointed to the stage. She told Sister Rita Mary, who was on the other wireless mic, something while pointing to me. I went on the stage and began to speak using the mic: "Hello, everyone! I am so glad to be here." I noticed that no one was paying attention to me. There was a lot of talk going on. Sister was still on the stage brandishing her own wireless mic, so I couldn't be heard. At that time Surinder, almost in tears, ran on the stage and told me she was sorry, but they had no time for me. Sister Rita Mary had ordered the technician to turn my mic off. I smiled a mock smile and gave the mic to her and walked down the stage steps. My broad smile must have cried on my face as I walked with Surinder out of the auditorium.

This was a great experience for me. While I couldn't make my ten-minute pitch for having deaf teachers of the deaf and about using ISL for teaching, I knew there were lots of teachers who understood these needs. I felt sure the day was not far when the annual national conference of teachers of the deaf will have a deaf president. You cannot violate human rights for too long!

My appearance there was not in vain. The following year, the local host of the same conference sent me an e-mail and worked closely with me to build the program, including inviting several deaf people and providing interpreters. However, the national president got wind of this and cancelled the conference for that year. I learned that in 2008, they did hire one interpreter and had one deaf teacher participate in that conference.

In July 2010, I was invited by the government of India to attend a meeting to help start the National Institute of Sign Language Studies. I flew to New Delhi and worked with the committee that the government had formed. I saw some of those who had refused to let me speak at that conference in 2006 sitting there as "experts on Indian Sign Language." They had jumped the bandwagon very quickly. I did not mind. It was my bandwagon.

43
Moving Up the Ladder

THE CALLS FOR INTERVIEWS BEGAN TO FILTER IN. AFTER two interviews, I found myself at the Illinois School for the Deaf (ISD) as its assistant superintendent. This was perhaps the first school that had both top positions held by Deaf persons. Pete Seiler had become the superintendent there only a few months earlier. I enjoyed working with him. Even though the two top positions were occupied by Deaf persons, all the other administrators were hearing.

The ISD had been one of the largest deaf schools in the country and had as many as seven hundred students living right on campus. After about 150 years of management by the traditional hearing white men, William Johnson, a hard of hearing man, became its superintendent in 1970s. However, Dr. Johnson could hear and speak, so his deafness wasn't noticed. He was followed by Dr. Lawrence Stewart, who was also deaf. Pete Seiler was, in fact, the third deaf superintendent. No other school had the distinction of having three deaf superintendents in a row.

Pete Seiler was big on bilingual education, which I had begun to support. The department principals strongly believed in the traditional method of using SimCom. However, this didn't cause any friction. We openly discussed both sides without any hostility. It was like two boxers going around and around waiting for an opening.

The times were changing at ISD. Not only were there two Deaf administrators, but there was also a female administrator. Joan Forney, a hearing white woman, was the principal of the elementary school. She was totally shunned by the seven or so male principals and assistant principals. Once I asked Joan to have lunch with me and I saw the look of shock on her face. I couldn't place it at that time, but during lunch she told me that this was the first time a male administrator had eaten lunch with her. I realized that she was also a minority.

Addressing a group of parents at the Illinois School for the Deaf, 1991.

However, I couldn't stay at ISD for long. I got a call from Eastern North Carolina School for the Deaf (ENCSD) asking me to apply for the superintendent's position there. I said no. I didn't want to change jobs that fast. I wanted to work for about five years at ISD before moving on. I also recalled that I had applied for the job about three years earlier and never even received a letter acknowledging my interest. Now times had changed and changed quickly.

After thinking again, I decided to go ahead and apply, explaining to Nirmala it would give me experience in being interviewed. She liked Jacksonville, Illinois, for its small, friendly community and moving again was just out of the question in her mind. She asked what would happen if I got the job. I told her not to worry; I wouldn't get it. The competition was tough.

I flew in to Raleigh the next week and drove over to Wilson for an interview. I learned that Frank Turk had also applied and had interviewed a couple of days before me. Frank Turk was dean of the Preparatory Department at Gallaudet when I was a freshman. I didn't think I had any chance competing against such a famous Deaf leader, but I was there already and went ahead with the interview.

The ENCSD interview committee was the largest I had ever faced. There were about twenty people. When I entered, I noticed almost all of them looked amused. They were smiling. First it puzzled me, but then I remembered that it was a Southern state. How did they view a short, deaf man from India? Their smile answered that question. It was obvious they weren't going to pick me. I just didn't fit the description of a school CEO—tall, white, hearing. I was short, dark, and deaf.

This made me reckless, which in turn gave me a lot of self-confidence. Gone was the nervousness and took off my jacket with "I can sign better without it" and threw it on an empty chair. I sat down on the chair, rubbed my palms together, and moved my eyes over the whole committee with a "let's have it" smile. I answered all the questions with flourish and impressed myself with my own knowledge. I kept gaining more confidence as I saw the expressions on their faces change from mocking smiles to seriousness to awe. At the end of the interview, I knew I had them.

The job offer came the very next day. Nirmala and I spent an hour discussing it. She was still against the move. Dheeraj didn't care and Neerja, who had already made a few close friends, supported her mother. I decided to ask Pete about his opinion. He said that I should go. You don't get such opportunities every day. Had Pete said, "Look, man, it is a great opportunity, but I need you here," I would have stayed at ISD. However, it was clear that Pete was happy to see me go. So I turned in my resignation and put the house on the market. It was April and I had to start working July 1.

I stayed at ENCSD for three years. It was my first experience as the head of a school. I wasn't actually the head—the power resided in Raleigh. The budget and human resources were directly under a government agency and the superintendent was more of an educational leader. This put me in an ongoing battle with the folks in Raleigh.

For example, when I had received the job offer from Raleigh, I had asked for a full-time interpreter and was promised that the interpreter "will be in place when I started my job." There was none when I arrived in Wilson. So I called Raleigh and asked about the interpreter or lack thereof.

My boss said, "On that. You know you have to hire one yourself."

That sounded simple enough.

"So a position has been added, so I can hire an interpreter?" I asked.

"No. You have to find the position of a teacher or other staff member and change it to interpreter's position," I was told.

This wasn't good. Direct services to students were the most important thing in my mind. The idea of "stealing" a teaching position didn't sit well with me. But I also needed an interpreter. After discussing the problem with the department principals, I found a vacant position and started the paperwork to get it changed to an interpreter. The bureaucratic wheels in Raleigh grind slowly and it took more than six months to get the paperwork approved and an interpreter hired.

During this process, my relations with Raleigh people began to sour. North Carolina had three schools for the deaf at that time. One was in Morganton, the original school over 150 years old. The second was ENCSD and third in Greensboro. I became good friend with Elmer Dillingham and Ron Wilson. We used to meet once a month to plan for joint curriculum and staff-development projects. However, we ended up discussing "Raleigh" issues most of the time. Both Elmer and Ron were real North Carolina boys and knew the bureaucratic rigmaroles and had developed a system to work with them. It was hard for me and I kept asking questions to the Raleigh people, which were obviously not appreciated.

The situation kept getting worse. It came to a head when the human resource director asked me to come to Raleigh for an interview. I thought it was about ENCSD personnel; however, it was about my immediate supervisors in Raleigh. They weren't following rules and Human Resources grilled me about what I knew. I had to be honest and told them how things were being managed. It was a "confidential" interview, but everything I said was relayed to my immediate supervisors. One didn't have to be a genius to figure out who was ratting them out.

This got me on their special list. Things kept getting worse and one morning, out of the blue, three of my supervisors came from Raleigh and I was given a pink slip with a few hours to clear out. I was happy about it and thought that it was a good ending and began to plan for the future.

However, the media didn't want me to go silently. The television news and the newspapers took over the case. It was a quiet time and the firing of a school superintendent made a great story. The very same evening, the Raleigh television stations ran the story and the next morning the banner in the *Wilson Times* was about it also. They tried to interview me but I declined. However, they interviewed staff members and some even began to write letters to the editors. All were supportive of me and the newspapers also got hold of my latest evaluation giving me excellent reviews. How could they let go of someone who was doing a great job? The editorial in the *Wilson Times* asked the state government to leave the school administration alone. This was a very strong editorial. Incidentally, the editor got an award for that editorial later.

After about a month, all of this hoopla died. However, my supervisors in Raleigh were forced to offer me another job, which I declined to accept. I had decided to take a "sabbatical" from work and stay home. I wrote to my contact in the CIA to increase my translation work. I had been translating Urdu, Hindi, and Punjabi newspaper stories and articles for their research division since I was a student. However, due to my full-time work, I was able to accept only small assignments. He was happy and soon I was translating Urdu and Hindi articles into English full-time. I was making almost the same amount of money by staying at home and translating a few hours daily than working full-time as a superintendent.

Teaching a class at the New Mexico School for the Deaf (NMSD).

Visiting a class at NMSD.

I thought about working as a translator and writing while staying at home, but after a couple of months the itch to work with people began to bug me and I wanted to get out of the house. Soon I began to send applications out.

In June, six months after being let go in Wilson, I got five job offers, all within twenty-four hours. That was a surreal experience. After considering the offers, I settled on the New Mexico School for the Deaf.

On July 1, I found myself in Santa Fe as superintendent of NMSD. It was like I had died and gone to heaven. The NMSD was governed differently than the ENCSD. The superintendent, who reported to a five-member board of regents appointed by the governor, had full responsibility for human resources and the budget. It took me a while to get used to being a superintendent in the real sense.

In Santa Fe, I expected the same. I asked where to call for a new position and learned I had to talk to the director of human resources and his office was right there. I called him and told him about my need for an interpreter and what I had to do about it.

"You hire one," he said matter-of-factly.

"What about paperwork and getting permission for creating this position?" I asked.

"I will do the paperwork and you have to give the permission," he said.

I had an interpreter within a week.

Working with the board of regents was another story. Each of them had their own private agenda. How effective a board is depends on the chairman. The chairman was strong and believed that the role of the board was to approve policy and the budget and support the superintendent in running the school things would go smoothly. The key wasn't to interfere in the superintendent's duties.

It didn't work that way most of the time. One board member's daughter taught in the school. She had been fired a few years earlier and was reinstated after he pulled some political high strings. And his main goal was to keep her in that position. Another one was a neighbor of an employee who wasn't exactly the best employee but had convinced the board member that he should be promoted to a higher position. Another

With a state senator, the school staff, and Dr. Deldgardo at NMSD.

Crowning the
homecoming queen.

board member's daughter was a student and she listened to everything her daughter told her—real or imaginary.

Thus, while as the superintendent I had the full authority on the budget and human resources, most of my energies were focused on responding to the board members' questions and demands for clarification of any action I took. I had to demote one administrator for a valid reason. But one board member decided to use this action to attack me. It took a lot of paperwork and formal and informal hearings before the case was put to rest.

Then there was the legislature. In North Carolina, the superintendents weren't allowed to testify for the budget or other needs in the legislature. In New Mexico, the superintendent had the full responsibility for lobbying the legislature. This wasn't a one- or two-month job but a year-round affair. I was fortunate in getting full support from the legislature. My deafness worked for me. This was the first time they had a deaf person coming to the legislative committees and the full house hearings. I got their full attention. While they grilled other educational heads, they didn't ask me any questions. Instead, they would make comments on how they must support the budget for the "deaf school."

44

Terms of Impairment

DEAF PEOPLE USED TO BE JUST THAT: DEAF. IN INDIA, THEY were known as deaf and dumb in 1967. This term didn't refer to a deaf person's intelligent level; it just pointed to his inability to speak. At Gallaudet, I learned that "dumb" in English means stupid and it was dropped a long time ago. I wrote to my friends in Delhi about it and they worked on changing the organization's name from "Deaf and Dumb Association to "Delhi Association of the Deaf." Little did I know how many changes in the nomenclature were to going to occur.

Recognition of ASL and Deaf culture has led to diversification within the Deaf community. In 1988, Deaf people wanted a Deaf president. In 2006, they protested against the selection of Dr. Fernandes, as the president of Gallaudet University, because that she was "not deaf enough." This sounded a pretty ambiguous term, so I Googled it at that time and got over 2,500 hits. There was even a book titled *Not Deaf Enough*.

The "deaf" were simply "deaf" or "hard of hearing" until the 1970s, when we were labeled "hearing impaired." This term, according to those who used it, encompassed all people with any kind of hearing problem. However, the novelty of this grandiose term faded fast. This was also the time when deaf identity along with the concept of ASL as a bona fide language was taking shape; thus the term "hearing impaired" was rejected by the Deaf community. "We are deaf," it declared, "not impaired anywhere." The term died its natural death in America but is very popular abroad—just like Marlboro cigarettes.

The burgeoning Deaf community, like any minority, began to stratify itself. Not all deaf people are alike and soon there were labels for various subgroups that composed the D/dcaf community. Many people take credit for the nomenclature for the four subgroups identified within the deaf community. Since no one has filed copyright for authorship, I will leave this issue alone and simply say that Deaf people coined these terms.

The first group, of course, is Deaf with the capital D. They have their own cultural and linguistic identity. Their families and friends are Deaf. Their contact with the hearing community is limited to working with them or living in their neighborhoods or associating with parents and siblings who happened to be hearing. This group considers itself to be the pure "Brahman Deaf" group and calls one another "deafies."

The second group is deaf people who are "audiologically deaf," but who don't consider themselves to be culturally deaf. This group comprises persons who are late deafened, associate with hearing people, and use Signed English. According to deafies, this group is not "really deaf" or not deaf enough, because its members think and act like hearing people. This group is labeled heafie—half deaf, half hearing. The sign for heafies is the same as hearing, except the place of sign is in front of the forehead. The deafies consider heafies as outsiders as Muslims are to Christians.

The next group is hearing people who by birth or by association have binding ties with the Deaf community. Hearing children of deaf couples (codas), hearing family members of families with a large number of deaf people, some interpreters, and those who work closely with the deaf and, more importantly, think like them are known as "dearies." They are hearing, but they think like deaf people, use ASL fluently, and socialize with the Deaf most of the time. Of course, dearies, despite their hearing, are more accepted in the Deaf community than the heafies despite the fact that they are hearing.

Then there is the vast majority. That is hearing people. No need to define them. They make up 99.99 percent of the world population. They are simply "hearies." They may sign or not and they may love deaf people or not. They are just hearies.

Deafness is a low-incident disability. We are a very small minority and since our disability is invisible, the general public recognizes us only when we use signs (or, perhaps, carry a sign proclaiming deafness). Since we are small, we need to be united. Every member of the Deaf community has to work together. This unity was visible in 1988 when, according to Jack Gannon, the world heard Gallaudet.

Since then, we have been fragmenting. This fragmentation hurts us. We blame hearing people for not being tolerant, but we have become intolerant ourselves. The vicious language dished out by bloggers shows how wide the depressing rifts are among us.

Deaf is deaf. When I arrived in America, we did talk about "those hard of hearing" people who sat on the fence. However, that didn't cause any rift.

45

Up in Smoke!

THE NUMBER OF SMOKERS IN THE UNITED STATES HAS gone down dramatically during the last few decades. When I arrived here in 1967, almost everyone smoked. Now, smokers are an exception. Most people either do not smoke or are in the process of quitting. Helping people quit smoking has become a billion dollar industry. I also, finally, quit smoking.

I started smoking when I was thirteen. Smoking in Gagret meant being a man and being macho. And in Gagret, almost everyone was macho and, therefore, smoked. Only a few didn't. It started when Ramesh visited Gagret during the summer as usual. He boasted that he had started smoking and needed his fix. I had not smoked yet but didn't want to sound backward, so I told him I also had started smoking. Of course, a thirteen-year-old boy couldn't smoke in public, even in Gagret. We had to find a place to smoke and, before that, we had to buy cigarettes.

Since everyone knew everyone else in Gagret, buying a cigarette (one could buy one cigarette instead of a pack in Gagret) wasn't easy. The few shops that sold cigarettes were owned by older people who would either refuse to sell a cigarette to us or report it to Babuji. So we had to case various shops and when we saw one being manned by a young guy, we ran to him, took out a paisa, and bought one cigarette. Holding it in safely between two palms, we ran all the way home. I stayed outside while Ramesh stole a matchbox from the kitchen. Then we ran again about half a mile to a safe place in the hills and had our smoke. The cigarette, soggy and bent from all the travels, lasted less than half a minute as we took turns at dragging at it. We choked, coughed, and had tears in our eyes from our efforts. Being macho was not easy.

Of course, we got hooked. I used to buy one cigarette and smoke it. Soon, it was a pack. I smoked for the next thirty-two years. However,

I was a sporadic smoker. I used to quit smoking on the New Year's Eve for one year and start the next New Year's Eve. I liked to smoke but didn't like the cost and knew of its ill effects on health. So this practice of smoking on alternate years was to keep the bad habit and also get a reprieve.

When my son Dheeraj was a bit over one year old, he became very interested in my smoking ritual. He would pick up the pack and my lighter and bring to me. That bothered me. I felt like I was giving him a head start in smoking. So after discussing this situation with Nirmala, who was a staunch opponent of smoking, especially mine, I decided that I would stop smoking inside the house and smoke only when I was at work. Nirmala's idea was that I should quit. Period. I told her I would take the middle way.

After dinner, I would take out one cigarette and my lighter and go out. Dheeraj would insist on going with me. I would tell him to stay inside as it was cold (it was winter). He would accept grudgingly. I would go out, light the cigarette, and walk up and down the sidewalk that bordered the lawn. The lofty thought that I was protecting my son from a bad habit blew with the smoke when I saw him staring at me from the window. I moved my smoking boundary further. I would walk a few hundred yards from our home before lighting up. While it got me out of Dheeraj's sight, it began to bother me. I had a habit that I didn't want my son to form but was fine to have myself! I have to stop it, I told myself.

Neerja, my daughter, began to offer vocal opposition to my smoking once she learned in the first grade that smoking was bad for one's health. She began to bug me and got a lot of encouragement from her mother in this effort. We were living in Austin at that time. Once, while I was smoking in the garage due to rain, she stood by my side, chattering as usual. She asked when I was going to quit smoking. I told her the same day she was going to quit sucking her thumb. That was a stalemate. I got rid of her nagging for a while, however.

I got a lot of help in stopping smoking. It was the summer of 1985. Nirmala had gone to India to attend my niece's wedding in April. Dheeraj and Neerja stayed because they were still in school. The plan was for us to join her later when school ended. In July, we three set out from Austin. We had to change our plane in New York. Smoking was allowed in airports at that time as well as in airplanes. However, there were separate sections—smoking and nonsmoking. I got seats in the nonsmoking section to protect the kids from smokers.

We had to change planes in New York. I needed a smoke and, as usual, couldn't find my lighter. I looked around. Smokers have a strong brotherhood and love to light each other's cigarette. I saw a tall guy smoking while leaning on a railing and approached him with cigarette lodged between my index and middle fingers. He looked at me and looked away and kept smoking. That was a first for me. I asked him, "Can I have a light please?" He looked at me and looked away. I couldn't believe myself and thinking that due to noise in the airport, he couldn't hear me, raised my voice and asked for the light again. He ignored me again. It was really embarrassing, and I was wondering what to do when a lady who was sitting nearby and must have watched the whole drama stood up and offered her lighter. I lit up and to show the guy who had "insulted" a fellow smoker, I was the winner, I moved closer to him, leaned on the railing, and began to puff on my cigarette with gusto. I was smiling, but deep down I felt embarrassed about my behavior. It was childish, I thought.

As we got into the huge 747 plane for New Delhi, we sat in the row with five seats. Every hour, I would get up and make the two passengers sitting to my left get up, so I could go to the smoking section for my fix. Then I would return and make them stand up again. Neerja, who was seven then and having read about the evils of smoking, had the great opportunity to tell me something. Dheeraj also was uncomfortable but kept his counsel to himself. Neerja, however, had to express her opinion. On my third trip back from the smoking section, she confronted me.

"Daddy, you are bothering everyone again and again. Why do you not quit smoking?" This wasn't a question; rather, it was an order.

I sat in my seat quietly, pretending to read my book. However, my thoughts were elsewhere. I thought about the man in New York airport who had made me look like a beggar and now being a pain to my fellow passengers and a source of embarrassment to my children. And all of this for smoking, which wasn't good for my health!

An hour later, when the urge came for a smoke, I didn't get up. That was almost a quarter of a century ago; I have not smoked since then. The smoking sections in airplanes have disappeared, although, for some strange reason, the "No Smoking" sign stays lit. It always reminds me of my last cigarette on a plane. I obey the sign.

46

The Communication Revolution

DEAFNESS IS ALL ABOUT COMMUNICATION OR LACK thereof. In 1967, when I came to Gallaudet, I was amazed at the accessibility of communication despite my limited signing skills. However, this was only among those who could sign. When it came to communicating with nonsigners, the great communication void opened. We didn't have the benefits of the telephone. When a deaf person needed to make an appointment with a doctor or call a hearing person for whatever reason, he had to ask a hearing person to call. This was a pain, as even the nicest hearing person would make a fuss eventually. They were busy or had other things to do. Then there was the phone bill they had to pay. Hearing children of deaf adults had to start interpreting for their parents from early childhood. Deaf people were dependent for communication on hearing friends, who usually became former friends.

In the era before the TTY was introduced, we used to pop up at friends' homes unannounced and were used to people showing up while we were in the middle of dinner or had our bedroom door closed for some reason. Life was full of surprises, as it should be.

The arrival of the TTY in 1970 brought a revolutionary change in communication. Almost overnight, most of us became proud owners of these huge machines. This was high tech at that time. While it was fine for communicating people who had TTYs, we still had to depend on hearing people for calling other hearing people who didn't own TTY machines. This problem was solved with the relay system, first locally and then nationally. Deaf people were independent to communicate with anyone, anywhere in the world. We thought TTY was it, but we were wrong. The large TTY machines gave way to small electronic TTYs. Then, with the arrival of e-mail, TTYs began to disappear. There are still some TTYs around but most of them are gathering dust.

There are new inventions, new gizmos, and new problems! Early in 2000, I visited Gallaudet for a meeting. While walking through the campus, I had an odd feeling that something was wrong. I was used to seeing students signing to each other while going from class to class or building to building. I got an eerie feeling when I didn't see many students signing.

Instead, all of them were walking with their heads bowed, focused on something in their hands and their thumbs punching away at small gizmos as if they were playing Pac-Man. These students were so focused on their gizmos that some of them would walk into each other. They didn't apologize for these accidents; they just kept punching their little machines.

That was the advent of Wyndtell wireless communication tools. Things have gotten a lot worse since then. There are several new machines like BlackBerrys, Sidekicks, and what-not. These new machines not only send and receive messages but do such stuff as browse the Web, make relay calls, send and receive e-mail, and make coffee on the go. Every Deaf and deaf person carries one or other of these little doohickeys.

I stayed away from this as long as I could. One couldn't ignore these machines. They became a part of a deaf person's dress. I was invited to address a graduating class and met with the group on the evening before graduation. Each of them had their Wyndtells (that was before Sidekick had kicked in) strapped to their belts or to purse straps. They were shocked to learn that I didn't have one. They looked at each other and looked at me as if I had shown up in jeans at a formal only party. They did manage to make me feel inferior.

Once while on a consulting trip to California, I had to stay a couple of additional days and decided to visit some old friends. I asked one of the interpreters if she knew my friend's phone number. The interpreter said I should try to page him. When I said I didn't have one of those machines, the interpreter looked so shocked that I decided to get something to strap to my belt as soon as I got home. She whipped out her own Sidekick and sent out a message. Two minutes later, I was in touch with my friend and a lunch date was established. I was impressed.

I understood that these gizmos were important for communication, but I also felt that they were being used for unnecessary communication. Once at a meeting, the Sidekick of a young lady sitting next to me kept on vibrating every few minutes. She would smile each time and make a major event of reading and responding to each message. I asked her what the important messages were. It was her boyfriend. He told her he loved her and she had responded she loved him, too.

These machines could also be dangerous. I was on my computer and noticed a former assistant on AIM. I buzzed her and we began to talk. She told me how her job was a pain since no one carried their own weight and how dumb her new boyfriend was (even though he had bought a Sidekick to stay in touch with her). After about thirty minutes, she said bye and thanked me for keeping her company.

I was puzzled, "Are you not in your office?"

"No, I am driving," she beeped.

I was aghast. "You mean you were doing 60 miles per hour while punching on your machine and reading my responses?"

"No," she typed back, "I am doing 80."

I turned my AIM off. No. Never. I will *not* buy any machine that might endanger my life. Let them laugh at me.

However, like everyone else, I bought one, or rather, my kids bought one for me. I carry it with me all the time and try to convince my friends who do not have one to benefit from the communication revolution.

47

There Is More . . .

PEOPLE OFTEN ASK OTHERS TO SUMMARIZE THEIR EXPE-
rience in some job or visit to a place in one word. My forty-plus years in
the United States of America can be described in one word: great!

It has been a great journey since 1967. America is called the land of
opportunity. Looking back at my life here, I can say with a redundant
"yes" that I was given a lot of opportunities to realize my goals and
dreams. I took advantage of some and squandered many.

While herding cattle in Gagret, I had not grand, but grandiose, dreams.
Walter Mitty could have learned a few things from me. However, they
were dreams and desires. Never in my waking hours did I ever think of
achieving what I have achieved in real life.

Just like all of you, I've learned a lot. I had the great fortune of having some very smart people as friends. Dan, Gene, and Chuck have been
great role models for learning English and the way American. Margie
was a great tutor who patiently corrected my English without making me
feel inadequate. Kirk was great in inspiring in me the confidence I needed
to do things new. Don taught me about working hard and playing hard.
He lives by that motto. There were many other friends who ignored my
shortcomings and helped me recognize the qualities I had. They also saw
wisdom in my humor and encouraged it. The most important gift these
friends gave me was to accept me as I was and never let me feel I was
a foreign student and, later, an immigrant. I was an American just like
them and I felt home.

My family also reaped benefits from living here. Nirmala learned English and was able to work for several years. Dheeraj and Neerja both
had excellent educations and have done well. Nirmala and I used to
tease them about arranging their marriages in India. Their response was
always a resounding no. It was interesting that they both always had

American friends in school and in college. We wondered if they were going to marry an American. However, after finishing college, they began to make friends with people of Indian origin. They met many ABCD (American Born Confused Desis [Indian]) like themselves and were able to find their life mates. They both have recently married: Dheeraj to Archna and Neerja to Neel. These were not arranged marriages, but had we arranged it, they might have ended up marrying these very spouses.

My students often ask me if I faced discrimination as an East Indian and a deaf person. I respond with a resounding "no." I could not think of even one incident during the past forty-plus years when I felt discriminated against. How could, I ask them, a deaf person from another country who started as a freshman at Gallaudet University at age twenty-six and achieved more than most deaf Americans complain about discrimination? Perhaps I should talk about some kind of "preferred status!"

However, there was discrimination, which I did not feel at that time. I always blamed myself for any shortcomings. One example comes to my mind.

Almost all PhD students in our department used to get well-paid jobs before they finished their degrees. They used these paid jobs as their internship experience, a required activity for the degree. I was also hoping for a similar job offer. However, none came. At the advice of Dr. Delgado, I visited various campus deans and vice presidents. Each of them apologized for the lack of an available position and steered me to other administrators with the hint that he or she "has a position that is perfect for you." I was passed around like the proverbial buck. Finally, I gave up this wild goose chase and talked to Judy LeNard, who was Dr. Davila's assistant for long-range planning. Judy came up with a job that I could use for my internship. This was not a real job and paid half of what my classmates were paid. It was a humble pie that I ate with a smile.

My applications to various jobs all over the country were not even acknowledged, as I mentioned earlier. Vic Galloway rose above his colleagues and opened a door in which I stuck my foot and, later, the whole body. Even after proving my worth and having glowing reference letters from Texas, my applications to other schools for higher positions were ignored until 1988. The Deaf President Now protest made deafness a trump card that cut through race and ethnicity.

I have been in the field of education all my life. When I started out in

1973, I had great hopes about finding the holy grail of solving problems in deaf education. However, I got involved in daily lesson plans, teaching, and testing students. Just like all other teachers, I did not have the time or energy to learn more.

As an administrator, I got very busy in the process of administrating and the real goals of making sure "every student reaches his utmost potential" was never achieved. All schools have this statement in various forms, but few succeed, if any.

During the last two decades, however, for the first time, deaf education in the United States is showing some progress. I am not talking about oral schools as I know little or nothing about them. I am talking about students who grew up in schools where signing is permitted along with speech instruction.

The slow but sure change to bilingual education is making the difference.

More and more schools have joined the Center for ASL/English Bilingual Education and Research (CAEBER) led by Dr. Stephen Nover. Dr. Nover has been involved in this movement since late 1980s. At that time, most deaf educators had slowly jumped on the bilingual education bandwagon. However, most of them took an emotional approach or tried to start it without thoroughly understanding it. Nover took the language planning approach and worked slowly and painstakingly in finding the right path to educating deaf children. More than half of the schools for the deaf in the United States have joined the CAEBER and are observing signs of progress in their students over the year.

My own observations also support this premise. I have encountered many profoundly deaf students who are prelingually deaf but have almost perfect English. More than that, they demonstrate great critical thinking skills and have the confidence that was rare among deaf people during the 1960s when I came here. Their pride in their use of ASL and respect for it as their mother tongue shows. The old feeling that the "deaf cannot do it" has been replaced with the idea that the "deaf can do anything."

Things have changed for the better . . . and are still changing.

ACKNOWLEDGMENTS

This book could not have been possible without the help of many individuals. I can't list them all, but will try:

- to my wife, Nirmala, for her ongoing support
- to my children Dheeraj and Neerja for their understanding; their respective spouses, Archna and Neel, for encouraging me to keep writing
- to my guide, friend and philosopher, Gene Bergman, for reading it all, lauding the good parts, giving ideas, and being a cheerleader
- to Don Bangs, another friend who slogged through my writing and helped make it more readable
- to Deirdre Mullervy, editor, for pushing me and making sure I stayed on track
- And Donald Wallace for encouraging me to write again.

My apologies to those who have helped if I've missed their names.

A portion of the proceeds from this book will be donated to Discovering Deaf Worlds (DDW), a non-profit international deaf advocacy organization dedicated to empowering deaf and hard of hearing communities in developing countries. DDW strives to advance the capacity of local deaf communities around the globe to meet their social, educational and employment needs.

Madan Vasishta has served on DDW's Board of Directors since November 2009, and is the chair of DDW's Program Development Committee.

For more information, visit www.discoveringdeafworlds.org.